A Quick History of

GRAND LAKE

INCLUDING ROCKY MOUNTAIN NATIONAL PARK
AND THE GRAND LAKE LODGE

Michael M. Geary

This work is dedicated to the memory of
Ted L. James, Sr. and Ted L. James, Jr.

Cover photograph by Ted L. James, III

Published by Western Reflections, Inc.
PO Box 710
Ouray, CO 81427

Printed in the United States of America

Table of Contents

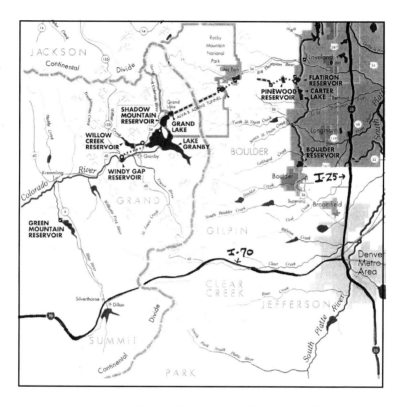

Area map showing Grand Lake in relationship to Denver and the Colorado Front Range, principal rivers of the region, and the major components of the Colorado-Big Thompson Project. (Courtesy Northern Colorado Water Conservancy District)

AUTHOR'S NOTE AND ACKNOWLEDGMENTS

This "quick history" does not attempt an in-depth analysis of Grand Lake's role in the profoundly complex issues that shaped the broad history of the American West, nor does it explore the fascinating geologic history of the region; these subjects are covered in other forums. Rather, this chronological narrative endeavors to give the reader a brief introduction and insight into the people and events that have influenced the human history of Grand Lake and its immediate vicinity. The narrative concludes with a short chapter on the history of the Grand Lake Lodge, a popular historic resort that has been a part of Grand Lake history since 1919.

A wide variety of individuals and institutions deserve recognition for their input and assistance during the creation of this book, including the staff of the Denver Public Library, Western History Collection; Joan Childers and Sybil Barnes of Rocky Mountain National Park; the Colorado Historical Society and the staff of the Stephen H. Hart Library; Pam Johnson and the Grand County Historical Museum; the Grand Lake Area Historical Society; the staff of Morgan Library and the Department of History, Colorado State University; the Fort Collins Public Library; and the Northern Colorado Water Conservancy District.

My sincere thanks to Bob Scott, Dorothy O'Ryan, Nancy Lavington, Aron Rhone, John Henry Rhone, Richard and Cathy Campbell, and the entire James family, especially Ted Sr., SueBee, Kathy, Ted III, and Reed, for their wonderful photos and memories of Grand Lake (thanks, Are Be, the next Guinness is on me). Thanks also go to Ken Jessen for his kind and timely words of advice, and to my dear friends and family in the Great Pacific Northwest. Finally, to my wife Kerri, who continues to astonish me with her inexhaustible wisdom and good humor, I give my love, deep respect, and most profound appreciation.

MIRROR IN THE MOUNTAINS

"Imagine a great mirror," wrote *Rocky Mountain News* founder and editor William Newton Byers, "a mile wide and two miles long, bordered all round with thick timber, and beyond that with stupendous mountains, flecked with patches and great fields of snow, except one narrow, scarce noticeable notch through which the river escapes, and you have Grand Lake." When Byers published his description in 1868, Grand Lake's total population consisted of a half-blind Civil War veteran named Joseph Wescott, who lived in a ramshackle log cabin nestled in the lodgepole pines on the west shore of the lake. No town existed on the north shore, no mining boom echoed across the Kawuneeche Valley, and certainly no sailboats raced for glory on the

Sunset on Baldy (Mt. Craig) reflected in the waters of Grand Lake, the "great mirror" described by William Newton Byers in 1868. (Author photo)

"great mirror." Much has changed in Grand Lake since 1868, but the lake and the trees and the lofty peaks remain virtually as Byers described them, effectively connecting contemporary Grand Lake with its long and storied past.

Located high in the Rocky Mountains at an elevation of 8,369 feet, Grand Lake is Colorado's largest natural body of water. Such a distinction may conjure images of immensity, of an enormous body of water covering many square miles. In reality, Grand Lake is rather diminutive as far as "largest" lakes go, an irregular ellipse roughly one mile wide by one and a half miles long, its 4.1-mile shoreline encompassing less than six hundred acres. Despite its comparatively small size, Grand Lake has been attracting humans to its shores for thousands of years, beginning with the early Paleo-Indians and continuing through subsequent Native American cultures who struggled for control of the region.

Grand Lake as seen from the 12,007-foot summit of Baldy, looking due west. Pioneer landscape photographer William Henry Jackson described the lake as an "irregular egg or pear shape" in 1874. (Author photo)

By the early decades of the nineteenth century, the lake and surrounding mountains hosted a variety of American and European explorers, trappers, and travelers. Eventually these newcomers displaced the region's indigenous populations and laid the foundations for the small town on the north shore of the lake that later gained fame as one of Colorado's oldest and most popular tourist destinations.

The exact origins of the name "Grand Lake" are a little vague. The Ute Indians who once wandered its shores called it *Ungarpakareter,* or Red Lake, probably because its cold, deep waters often glow with a crimson hue in the canted light of the Colorado sunset. Legend has it that the Utes also referred to the lake as "Spirit Lake," although confusion still exists over the exact source of this name. The Arapaho Indians (also spelled Arapahoe), mortal enemies of the Utes in both legend and reality, had a number of names for the lake, including *Ahbanthnaach* (Big Lake) and *Batannaach* (Holy or Spirit Lake). The Arapaho reference to "Spirit Lake" came from an ancient myth about an enormous supernatural buffalo that the Arapahos believed lived beneath the surface of the lake.

Spanish *conquistadores* searching for gold and glory began exploring the lower reaches of the Colorado ("red" or "ruddy") River in the middle 1500s, but the chronicles of this era offer little verifiable evidence that Spanish explorers actually followed the river to its headwaters near Grand Lake. Historian Robert Black contends that the name "Grand" is "obviously of French origin," perhaps bestowed by one of the adventurous French trappers who explored the region in the first half of the eighteenth century. A map drawn in 1839 by David H. Burr includes a wildly inaccurate depiction of the Grand River, leading to speculation that perhaps Burr played some role in naming the lake. Other sources give John Charles Frémont, the "Pathfinder of the West," credit for naming both Grand Lake and the Grand River in 1843 or 1844, although the historical accuracy of this claim is rather dubious, considering the lack of any references to Grand Lake in Frémont's journals. In 1863 Irish writer M. O'C.Morris referred to the lake as "Still-Water Lake." Grand Lake resident and local historian Carolyn Rhone gave early pioneer Joseph Wescott credit for naming the lake, while A. Phimister Proctor, who first visited Grand Lake in 1875, remembered yet another Indian name, "Meteor Lake," evidently because of the large number of meteors visible in the crisp mountain air. Proctor blamed the "fool whites" for changing the name to Grand Lake. President William Howard Taft called it simply "the most beautiful sheet of mountain water in the world."

Confusion over the names "Colorado River" and "Grand River" further clouds the issue of who actually named Grand Lake. The early Spanish referred to the river that carved the Grand Canyon as the Colorado, and most American maps of the middle 1800s generally utilized this name, with one important distinction: above its confluence with the Green River (near present-day Moab, Utah) the Colorado became the Grand. This designation may have inspired someone, perhaps an anonymous fur trapper or early map-maker, to christen the lake at the head of the river "Grand Lake." Maps continued to refer to the upper portion of the river as the Grand until 1921, when an astute Colorado politician named Edward Taylor persuaded Congress to designate the entire waterway as the Colorado River, in recognition of the state where the river begins its 1,450 mile journey to the Gulf of California.

Grand Lake's early recorded history reads like the screenplay for a classic Western film, complete with an astonishing collection of familiar characters and events: Indians and outlaws, shootouts and buried treasure, fur trappers and explorers, pioneer settlers and hard-rock miners, boom towns and broken dreams. More recently, Grand Lake witnessed the creation of one of the nation's most popular national parks. Later, the 265-foot-deep, glacier-carved lake became the centerpiece for one of the largest transmountain water diversion projects in the country. Since the arrival of the first Anglo-American trappers and explorers in the mid-nineteenth century, Grand Lake has also endured the continual ebb and flow of economic development, along with a succession of controversies concerning the use and abuse of natural resources and the disposition of public lands. In this respect, the history of Grand Lake is but one thread in a complex tapestry of regional and national history that encompasses not only Rocky Mountain National Park but also Middle Park, the state of Colorado, and ultimately the entire American West.

Right: Map of Grand Lake, drawn by Fred Jones, Jr., circa 1950. Locations of homes and businesses are represented by numbers along the shore; numbers within the lake correspond to water depths. (Courtesy James family, Grand Lake Lodge)

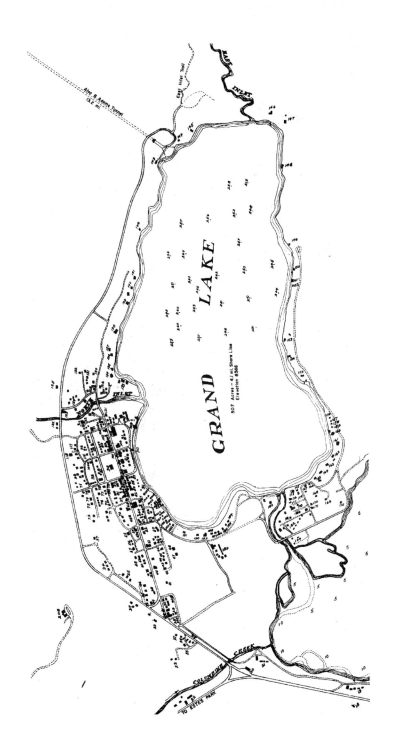

CHAPTER ONE

ANCIENT FOOTPRINTS

Modern scholars believe that the earliest human visitors to the Grand Lake region were Stone Age hunters associated with the Clovis culture, a term first used in 1932 after archaeologists discovered stone projectile points near Clovis, New Mexico. Subsequent archaeological discoveries suggest that the ancestors of the Clovis initially entered the North American continent by crossing the Bering Land Bridge sometime during the end of the last Ice Age, perhaps 25,000 years ago. As global temperatures warmed and the great continental ice sheets began retreating northward, centuries of migration brought these "Paleo-Indians" to what is now the state of Colorado, where they hunted mammoth and a large (now extinct) species of bison known as *Bison antiquus.*

Archaeologists have discovered projectile points, bone scrapers, and other stone tools associated with both the Clovis and subsequent Folsom cultures throughout Colorado, including the region that later became Rocky Mountain National Park (RMNP). Radiocarbon dating of projectile points found in the Trail Ridge region of the park indicates that Paleo-Indians may have traversed the crest of the Rockies sometime between 10,000 and 15,000 years ago. Since the high elevations (up to and above 12,000 feet) and often brutal weather of the Trail Ridge country are prohibitive to long-term habitation, the logical conclusion is that the Paleo-Indians undertook seasonal migrations across the mountains to exploit the rich hunting grounds on the west side of the Continental Divide, including those near Grand Lake. As the deep snows and bone-cracking cold of winter approached, the Paleo-Indians returned to the more temperate climate of the Front Range. Consequently, no evidence of permanent occupation by Paleo-Indians has ever been discovered in the Grand Lake area. Available evidence does suggest that the Paleo-Indians may have constructed the intriguing stone walls found at over forty locations along the crest of the Front Range, including one wall identified near the current route of Trail Ridge Road. Originally thought to be primitive "forts" used to defend territory, archaeologists now believe that the low stone structures are actually the remnants of game-drive systems used by the Paleo-Indians to herd animals towards predetermined "kill zones," where hunters waited to ambush their prey. Some of these walls date from as early as 4000 B.C., indicating a long tradition of Paleo-Indian activity in the area. Once constructed, the walls were utilized by generations of Indian hunters who sought concealment in a tundra environment that is conspicuously devoid of cover.

Prehistoric stone wall constructed by Paleo-Indians perhaps 5,000 years ago near the route of present-day Trail Ridge Road. One of forty-two such walls identified along the crest of Colorado's Front Range. Once thought to be primitive defensive structures, the walls are now recognized to be remnants of game-drive systems used to herd prey toward predetermined kill zones. Photo circa 1937. (Courtesy Rocky Mountain National Park Historical Collection, hereafter cited RMNPHC)

An interesting artifact discovered eight miles south of Grand Lake in 1922 suggests some intriguing origins for the region's earliest inhabitants, although noted historian Robert Black, author of *Island in the Rockies*, wrote rather forcefully that the artifact "may be disregarded." Rocky Mountain National Park Superintendent Roger Toll's official report from August 31, 1922 described how a man identified only as "Chalmers" uncovered the object while "making an excavation for earth." The artifact in question was stone, about sixteen inches tall, weighed approximately sixty pounds, and had obviously been carved by human hands to resemble "a grotesque figure of a man." Vaguely Aztec or Mayan in appearance, the figure included carvings of a "long-tusked mammoth" and some "prehistoric animals of the lizard family", as well as "a number of hieroglyphics." Toll reported that "the Smithsonian Institution is investigating the find, which is authentic as far as can be learned, although there are several incredible aspects." The report contained no additional information on the artifact, and its true origin remains a mystery.

Evidence in the form of ancient firepits, burned bones, grinding stones, and scattered remnants of stone tools dating from circa 2500 B.C. offers ample proof that early Native Americans hunters, just like their Paleo-Indian ancestors, continued to visit the Grand Lake region on a recurring, seasonal basis for centuries. Arrowheads found in Rocky Mountain National Park suggest that sometime between A.D. 450 and 600, nomadic hunters introduced the bow and arrow to the region. Excavations conducted in 1948 in areas scheduled to be flooded by Lake Granby uncovered bones, pot shards, and tools dating from circa A.D. 900 to A.D. 1300. These artifacts exhibited characteristics linking them with both the pre-Columbian hunting cultures of the Great Plains as well as the Desert Cultures of the Southwest, but again, no evidence of permanent occupation by Paleo-Indians has surfaced at any site in the vicinity of Grand Lake. By the time the Spanish *conquistadores* began probing the extreme

Prehistoric stone artifact excavated eight miles south of Grand Lake in 1922. The sixteen-inch figure weighed approximately sixty pounds and included carvings of lizards, a long-tusked mammoth, and various hieroglyphics. Origin unknown.
(Courtesy RMNPHC)

southern reaches of the Rocky Mountains in the mid-1500s, the Paleo-Indians, who had spent centuries hunting in the region that later became Rocky Mountain National Park, had long since given way to the Native American cultures that played a prominent role in the history of Grand Lake: the Ute, Arapaho, and Cheyenne.

Exactly when these tribes first appeared in what is now Colorado is unknown. Some historians (as well as ethnologists, archaeologists, and anthropologists) suspect that the Native Americans who frequented pre-Columbian Colorado were merely the descendants of earlier Paleo-Indian cultures who had lived in the region. Other scholars believe that these early inhabitants were the descendants of the Anasazi, who dominated the Four Corners region for centuries until their culture disintegrated around A.D. 1300. While the debate over the true origins of these tribes continues, most historians generally agree that the Utes controlled the mountains, mesas, and parks of Colorado's high country during the period of contact with Spain's New World empire. By the beginning of the 1700s, the Utes were at the height of their power.

Known variously as the Utahs, Uticahs, Yutta, or "Blue Sky People," the Utes acquired Spanish horses perhaps as early as 1626, and French firearms by at least the 1750s. Access to horses and guns fundamentally transformed the Utes and other Native American cultures by providing greater mobility and firepower, which in turn increased the likelihood of a successful hunt. Horses also increased contact between rival tribes, while firearms virtually guaranteed deadly consequences for such contact. By 1790, under pressure from the expansionist Sioux tribes, the Arapaho Indians (called "Saretika" or "Dog Eaters" by the Shoshoni and Comanche) fled their traditional territory in the Black Hills and moved to the Front Range region of the Colorado Rockies. Shortly thereafter, the Arapaho and their allies, the Cheyenne, began a protracted war with the Ute Indians. The hostility between these tribes forms the basis for the most enduring legend in the long and colorful history of Grand Lake, a widely known and oft-repeated tale about a fierce battle, some fragile rafts, and a sudden, deadly storm.

CHAPTER TWO

THE LEGEND OF GRAND LAKE

"White man, pause and gaze around,
For we tread now on haunted ground!"
So said a chief to me one day,
As along the shore we wound our way.
—Judge Joseph L. Wescott,
The Legend of Grand Lake, circa 1882

Grand Lake's first permanent resident, Joseph L.Wescott, claimed that during his initial visit to the lake in 1867, he encountered an old Ute Indian camping near the shore. Isolation and a lack of other visitors virtually ensured that Wescott and the Indian would become friends, and they eventually began spending their evenings together, engaged in long conversations in the flickering light of a campfire. It was during one such conversation that the Indian told Wescott about an epic battle that had occurred on the shores of Grand Lake, long before Europeans or Americans had ever set foot in the region.

According to the Indian, a tribe of Utes had established a camp near the edge of the lake, where they planned to spend the summer taking full advantage of the area's excellent fishing and hunting opportunities. To ensure the safety of the camp, the Utes positioned scouts on the large rock outcropping just west of the lake. From this vantage point, known to contemporary visitors as Scout Rock or Lookout Point, the Ute scouts enjoyed a commanding view of the surrounding countryside. One night, as twilight settled over the lake, an enormous thunderstorm suddenly appeared over the Never Summer Mountains to the west, shattering the sky with flashes of lightning and great screaming peals of thunder. Terrified by the deafening din, the Ute scouts abandoned their post and sought shelter from the gathering storm.

Meanwhile, unbeknownst to the Utes, a raiding party consisting of Cheyenne and Arapaho warriors had left the sprawling plains of eastern Colorado, crossed the Continental Divide at Thunder Pass, and made their way down the Kawuneeche Valley with plans to attack (Kawuneeche is an Arapaho word meaning "coyote;" this valley was also known as the "Valley of Plenty Jerked Elk Meat" and, more recently, the North Fork). Using the storm to conceal their approach, the raiders crept to within sight of the Ute camp. As dark curtains of drenching rain finally reached the lake, the Cheyenne and Arapaho warriors unleashed a furious barrage of arrows, accompanied by a chorus of shrieking battle cries. Surprised by the initial assault, the Utes quickly recovered and launched their own salvo of deadly arrows. In the ensuing chaos, the Utes gathered all of their women and children, placed them on a handful of small rafts and

The view from Scout Rock, looking southwest toward what used to be the Colorado River valley. Ute Indian scouts used this site as a lookout post while camping near Grand Lake. Shadow Mountain Lake, part of the Colorado-Big Thompson Project, inundated the valley in the late 1940s. (Author photo)

logs that had been beached along the shore, and set them adrift on the cold, black water.

The tempest grew stronger, threatening to tear the sky open. Merciless blasts of icy wind twisted and howled across the lake, churning the water into a roiling cauldron of white-capped fury. Still the battle raged, strewing the ground with fallen warriors. Finally the carnage reached a climax. As the last remnants of the Ute forces rallied to drive the invaders from the field, they realized to their horror that the storm had overturned the rafts and logs, drowning all of their women and children. Forever after, the Utes avoided Grand Lake entirely. They considered the area to be hope-lessly haunted, and legend has it that the ghostly phan-toms of their dearly departed can be seen in the spectral mists that often rise above the lake on summer mornings.

The spectral mists of Grand Lake. Ute Indians believed these vapors were the spirits of women and children who drowned during a fierce battle on the shores of the lake. Joseph Wescott immortalized the battle in his epic 1882 poem The Legend of Grand Lake. *(Courtesy Jim Colombo)*

The legend also claims that during the winter, the terrifying shrieks and moans of the dead Utes can be heard echoing beneath the surface of the frozen lake. Yet another legend claims that Grand Lake's trout all have red-colored flesh from the blood of the dead Indians.

Years later, Joseph Wescott enlisted the aid of John Barbee, an educated Kentuckian and itinerant prospector then living in the region, and together (although Wescott alone is generally given credit) they wrote a long poem entitled *The Legend of Grand Lake*, which describes the battle in great detail, including the names of some of the principal participants: Chekiwow and Black Eagle led the Utes, while Red Wolf and Black Bear commanded the enemy raiding party. The poem also makes reference to a possible date for the battle: "Thirty-four years have sped away, since the close of that fatal day," which, if Wescott's version is to be believed, means the battle took place sometime during the summer of 1833.

Grand Lake's first newspaper, *The Prospector*, published the entire poem in July 1882, and ever since people have assumed that the tale told to Wescott by the Indian chief was the source for the name "Spirit Lake." Curiously, the epic poem makes no specific references to "Spirit Lake," although it does include a verse that contemplates "how many of our brave band, next morn will be in Spirit land," and another that proclaims "Henceforth let this be haunted ground, where evil spirits may abound." According to historian C.W. Buchholtz, author of the definitive history of Rocky Mountain National Park, Wescott's poem may contain certain elements of truth, or it could be "mere wishful thinking on the part of settlers who hoped the Utes would not return. They preferred the legend over the reality of worrying about being attacked."

At any rate, the legend continued to grow. Mary Lyons Cairns published *The Legend of Grand Lake* in its entirety in her landmark history of Grand Lake, but the shortened version is familiar to virtually every resident of Grand Lake,

9

who evidently see little reason to alter a good story for the sake of historical accuracy. In reality, the Utes never specifically referred to Spirit Lake, preferring the name Red Lake. Credit for the name Spirit Lake should instead be given to Arapaho mythology. It seems that one winter long ago, after the lake had almost completely frozen over, a group of Arapaho Indians noticed a series of large buffalo tracks emanating from a hole in the ice near the center of the lake. The tracks also appeared to return to the hole, leading the Indians to conclude that an enormous, supernatural buffalo must live in the lake. This legend became the basis for the name Spirit Lake.

An interesting footnote to this story concerns an effort to clarify the names of geographic features in the Grand Lake/Estes Park region. In July 1914, six months before President Woodrow Wilson signed legislation creating Rocky Mountain National Park, members of the Colorado Mountain Club arranged for a small delegation of Arapaho Indians from the Wind River Reservation in Wyoming to be brought to Estes Park, with hopes that they could provide Indian names for the region's mountains and valleys. These "authentic" names would then be used for official maps of the proposed national park. The delegation consisted of two old Indians who were familiar with the Estes Park area, seventy-three-year-old Gun Griswold and sixty-three-year-old Sherman Sage, as well as a mixed-blood Arapaho named Tom Crispin, who came along as an interpreter. The small group, accompanied by local guides Shep Husted and Oliver Toll, set out from Estes Park on horseback for a two-week trip that took them over the Continental Divide, down the North Fork (Kawuneeche) Valley to Grand Lake, then back to Estes via Flattop Mountain and Bear Lake.

When they reached Grand Lake, the Arapahos were asked if they remembered the great battle with the Utes. They did, but their memory of the conflict differed considerably from the Ute version of events. Sage and Griswold insisted that there had been a minor skirmish just

Members of the 1914 Arapaho Indian Trip sponsored by the Colorado Mountain Club to ascertain Indian names for geographic features in the Grand Lake/Estes Park region. From left to right: Shep Husted, Estes Park guide; Gun Griswold, Sherman Sage, and Tom Crispin, Arapaho Indians from the Wind River Reservation in Wyoming; Oliver Toll, trip chronicler; and (seated) David Hawkins. (Courtesy RMNPHC)

west of the lake in an area known as the Sagebrush Flats, near where the current post office and elementary school are located, and that the Ute forces were driven up the slope of Shadow Mountain, which the Arapahos called Echo Mountain. Far from the bloody carnage described in Wescott's poem, however, the Arapahos recalled that the total Ute casualties were one man, two women, and a baby. Moreover, they remembered nothing about any rafts that had overturned on the lake, nor the violent thunderstorm. Finally, interpreter Tom Crispin explained that two of the Arapahos who were supposedly killed during the battle, Red Wolf and Black Bear, in fact died some years later; Pawnee Indians killed Red Wolf near Cheyenne, and U.S. soldiers killed Black Bear nine miles east of Lander, Wyoming.

Despite the discrepancies between the Ute and Arapaho versions of the battle, most historians agree that the basis for the legend is accurate: the Utes and Arapahos (as well as the Cheyenne and other tribes) did engage in conflicts in the Grand Lake region, and continued to do so well into the middle of the nineteenth century. One early eyewitness, Charlie S. Strobie, reported that a skirmish between the Utes and a force of Arapaho and Cheyenne warriors had taken place near Grand Lake as late as 1866. Still, beyond the Indian names and legends, scattered arrowheads, and crumbling ruins of an old Indian fort discovered near Granby, little hard evidence remains to indicate the presence of Utes and Arapahos in Grand Lake. By the early 1800s, the arrival of European and American explorers and fur trappers signaled the beginning of the end for the Indians who had hunted in the Grand Lake region for centuries. These new arrivals had little tolerance for the lifeways of the area's indigenous populations, and toward the end of the nineteenth century, efforts were underway to remove the Indians from the area permanently.

CHAPTER THREE

TRAPPERS AND TRAILBLAZERS

History has failed to record the names of the first Europeans to visit Grand Lake. Spanish expeditions of the late sixteenth and early seventeenth centuries may have explored the Colorado River all the way to its source near Grand Lake, but no chronicle exists to verify such a journey.

French trappers and traders almost certainly penetrated deep into the Colorado Rocky Mountains by at least 1724, yet since these early entrepreneurs were notorious for being either illiterate or tight-lipped at best, they left behind few records of their travels. The Louisiana Purchase of 1803, coupled with the burgeoning fur trade, encouraged extensive American exploration in the region that later became Colorado. American trapper James Pursley (also known as Purcell) is known to have explored the Rockies in search of beaver and gold as early as 1805, shortly before Zebulon Pike undertook his famous exploration of what became southern Colorado. Between 1811 and 1817, fur trappers associated with the Missouri trade explored most of the rivers and streams of the Colorado Front Range. While it is certainly conceivable that at least one of these intrepid trappers stumbled upon Grand Lake during the relentless quest for fur, no record exists to confirm such a discovery.

By the time Stephen H. Long's official U.S. government expedition reached the Rocky Mountains in 1820, French trapper Joseph Bessonet (aka Bijeau) had traversed the region "in almost every direction." Hired by Long as a guide and hunter, Bijeau was able to describe in great detail the region known collectively as the Colorado park country, a series of vast, open basins (North, Middle, and South Parks) that punctuate the rugged interior of the Colorado Rockies. Since Grand Lake is one of the most prominent features of Middle Park, it is almost inconceivable that Bijeau knew nothing of its existence. Still, the records from Long's expedition make no mention of the lake.

In 1839, a small group of travelers led by Thomas Jefferson Farnham passed through Middle Park on their way to Oregon, inspiring Farnham to produce what is perhaps the first written description of the region:

> The valleys that lie upon this stream and some of its tributaries are called by the hunters "The Old Park." If the qualifying term were omitted, it would be well described by their name. Extensive meadows running up the valleys of the streams, woodlands skirting the mountain bases and dividing the plains...a splendid park indeed; not old, but as new as the first fresh morning of creation.

As enchanting as Farnham obviously found Middle Park, one wonders what his eloquent pen would have produced if he and his fellow travelers had visited Grand Lake. Since their travels only took them through the extreme western portions of the Park, they left the region without ever setting eyes upon the pristine lake situated beneath the lofty peaks of the Continental Divide.

Past historians occasionally succumbed to the temptation to link such renowned explorers of the American West as John Charles Frémont, Jim Bridger, and Kit Carson with the discovery of Grand Lake. While it is true that Frémont passed through Colorado in 1844, records of his travels lack any specific reference to Grand Lake. His journals do make clear, however, that he was quite familiar with both North and Middle Parks:

> The appearance of the country in the Old (Middle) Park is interesting, though of a different character from the New (North Park); instead of being a comparative plain, it is more or less broken into hills, and surrounded by the high mountains, timbered on the lower parts with quaking asp and pines.

Shortly after crossing Muddy Pass in the western portion of the Park, Frémont and his party encountered a group of two hundred Arapaho and twenty Sioux who were hunting and spoiling for a fight with the indigenous Utes. After a few tense moments, "with something more than the usual amount of presents," Frémont managed to avoid a conflict, then prudently retreated towards South Park and the Great Plains. If he did visit Grand Lake, his journals failed to mention it.

Kit Carson, one of Frémont's guides during his 1844 expedition, is often credited with exploring the entire territory around Longs Peak. According to historian C.W. Buchholtz, such claims "might also be wishful thinking on the part of those who hoped to forge a link with a legend." If Carson did in fact explore the area around Grand Lake, he left no record of it. Nor did Jim Bridger, the famous mountain man who guided Irish nobleman Sir St. George Gore during a hunting expedition into Middle Park in 1854. Lord Gore, equipped with an astonishing array of men and material, including more than one hundred horses, twenty oxen, fifty hunting hounds, and forty men, spent three months slaughtering game in Middle Park. Gore gave his name to a number of geographic features in the western portion of Middle Park, including a rugged mountain range and a scenic mountain pass, but neither he or Jim Bridger left any records concerning Grand Lake.

Famous explorers, mountain men, and Irish barons notwithstanding, history generally fails to recognize anyone as the official European or American "discoverer" of Grand Lake. Countless anonymous trappers, hunters, and miners undoubtedly walked along its shores, but since none of them chose to remain in the area on a permanent basis, it is virtually impossible to specify who came first. Consequently, most of the books and articles dealing with the history of pioneer settlers in Grand Lake begin with Philip Crawshaw, simply because the letters he sent home to his family provide an authentic and verifiable historical record of his early presence in the region.

Crawshaw came to Grand Lake from Chillicothe, Missouri, in the summer of 1857. He constructed a small log cabin on the west shore of the lake and began trapping along the North Fork of the Colorado (Grand) River. Occasionally he shared his camp with other trappers, but by the time the deep snows of winter came, Crawshaw found himself alone. For five long months he endured the solitude. He spent his days tending to his traps, reaping a bountiful harvest of beaver, fox, and bobcat furs. When darkness fell he huddled alone in his cabin, confined by the frigid cold of the Rocky Mountain winter. Crawshaw stayed in the region until 1861, then decided that his destiny lay elsewhere. He packed up

One of the earliest images of Grand Lake, an unfinished watercolor by Georgetown minister William Phipps, who visited the lake in August 1868. Note the faint outline of a cabin (presumably Joseph Wescott's) and assorted burned trees. Such fire damage appears in a number of early photographs of Grand Lake. (Courtesy Denver Public Library, Western History Collection)

his furs and meager belongings, abandoned his cabin near the shore of Grand Lake, and traveled to the burgeoning frontier town of Denver, where he traded his furs for gold dust and set out across the plains, heading for Missouri. His good fortune soon ran out. Before Crawshaw reached his home in Chillicothe, a group of William Quantrill's notorious Confederate raiders relieved him of his precious gold dust. As far as can be determined, Crawshaw never returned to his cabin on the shores of Grand Lake.

Philip Crawshaw would be little more than a footnote in the history of Grand Lake were it not for a few small details: he is widely credited with building the first log cabin in Grand Lake, and by choosing to remain in Grand Lake during the long Rocky Mountain winter, he became the first American (of whom there is a record) to break the pattern of seasonal occupation that had been established as far back as the Paleo-Indians. Despite Crawshaw's early presence, Grand Lake remained far from the beaten path. Bitterly cold winters, the lack of suitable roads and trails in the immediate vicinity, and the lake's rather remote location hard against the western flank of the Continental Divide combined to discourage all but the most determined travelers.

The local Ute Indians also tended to discourage casual visitors. Although most early records portray them as friendly and willing to share their land, by the 1860s the Utes of Middle Park were beginning to resent the increasing numbers of foreigners in Middle Park, who they perceived as trespassers on their traditional hunting grounds. Sir George Gore's senseless slaughter of game animals in 1854 had deeply angered them, as did the gold-fevered miners who descended upon the region in the wake of the Pikes Peak Gold Rush of 1858-59. The U.S. government's official recognition of the new Colorado Territory on February 28, 1861, inspired even greater numbers of settlers to pour into the Rocky Mountains. After Edward L. Berthoud pioneered the new, "easily practicable" route known today as Berthoud

Pass into southern Middle Park in the spring of 1861, conflicts between the Utes and the new arrivals became increasingly common. Further hostilities seemed inevitable.

Still, Grand Lake managed to retain its isolated charm. Far from the turmoils of the Civil War, the feverish Pikes Peak Gold Rush, and the Indian troubles festering elsewhere in Middle Park, the mountains and rivers around Grand Lake continued to attract only scant numbers of trappers, fishermen, hunters, and miners, most of whom stayed only for the summer months. That all changed in June 1867, when a rheumatic, near-sighted Civil War veteran named Joseph L. Wescott arrived and established a homestead on the west shore of the lake.

CHAPTER FOUR

FAMOUS FIRSTS

Born in Nova Scotia in 1838, Grand Lake's first permanent resident spent most of his childhood in Michigan and Iowa. At age twenty, dazzled by exciting tales of the Pikes Peak Gold Rush, Joseph L. Wescott decided to head west and seek his fortune. By June 1860 he had arrived in the frontier boom town of Central City, where he stayed for nearly a year before moving on to Empire, on the eastern side of the soon-to-be discovered Berthoud Pass. Succumbing to the patriotic fervor sweeping the country following the outbreak of the Civil War, Wescott enlisted in the First Colorado Volunteers in September 1861. He served as a private in Company G, First Colorado Cavalry, until October 1864, when his frequent, painful bouts of inflammatory rheumatism compelled the army to muster him out. He returned to Empire, where in the spring of 1865 a fire consumed his small cabin and destroyed everything he owned except his trusty rifle.

Distraught over his loss and wracked with pain from rheumatism, Wescott joined a small party of travelers from Georgetown who were heading for Middle Park. Wescott had heard rumors about the remarkable healing powers of the Hot Sulphur Springs, and before long he found himself heading for Berthoud Pass, swinging precariously in a hammock that his companions had lashed between two burros. The travelers reached the springs in the early summer of 1865, and shortly thereafter Wescott decided to settle in the area. He constructed a small cabin, trained a young coyote as a guard dog, and began soaking in the soothing springs. Wescott gradually regained his health, and with renewed vigor he began fishing, trapping, and making friends with the local Ute Indians. When *Rocky Mountain News* owner/editor William Newton Byers arrived later that summer with plans to acquire, legally or otherwise, the springs and all of the land surrounding them, he found a stubborn Joseph Wescott already in residence.

Not to be deterred, Byers initiated a clever plan to seize control of the springs. He, too, constructed a small log cabin, installed his brother-in-law Jack Sumner as caretaker, and began weaving a tangled web of questionable surveys and dubious land trades to achieve his goal. However, Wescott and Sumner soon became good friends, which threatened to derail Byers' carefully crafted land-grab. The complex details of the shadowy plan are best explained elsewhere, but Wescott's role in the saga ended after Byers offered him $500 for his land holdings near the springs. Wescott accepted the offer and packed up his belongings, leaving Byers and Sumner to continue their scheming and dreaming.

With his health restored and his wallet fattened, Joseph Wescott left Hot Sulphur Springs in 1867 and headed for the shores of Grand Lake, twenty-six miles to the northeast.

Joseph Wescott, Grand Lake's first permanent resident and author of The Legend of Grand Lake. *Wescott arrived in 1867 and remained until his death in 1914. In 1888 he platted "Grand Lake City" on his 160-acre homestead on the west shore of the lake. His "city" failed to materialize, and town development continued on the north shore. Photo circa 1890.* (Courtesy Denver Public Library, Western History Collection)

A handful of hunters and fishermen had visited the lake since Philip Crawshaw's departure in 1861, but for all intents and purposes the region remained largely uninhabited, with Crawshaw's abandoned cabin the only evidence of human occupation. Enchanted with the solitude and the sublime vistas that surrounded him, Wescott simply appropriated Crawshaw's cabin, staked his claim to the 160 acres of land allowed under the 1862 Homestead Act, and settled in to become Grand Lake's first official permanent resident.

At some point during his tenure in Middle Park, Wescott acquired the nickname "Judge." Various historic sources attribute the nickname to a combination of Wescott's considerable intellect and his wizened, grizzled appearance, which made him seem much older than his thirty-plus years. Other explanations for the nickname stem from his position as Grand Lake's first official postmaster in 1877, or, as historian Caroline Bancroft claims, from his later service as a justice of the peace in Grand Lake. Whatever its origins, the nickname stuck, and Judge Wescott quickly became the lake's most famous character.

Using Crawshaw's crude dwelling as a temporary shelter, the Judge began building his own cabin nearby, on the west shore of the lake just south of the outlet. With ample timber at his disposal, he soon assembled a rather substantial structure, complete with a sloping, shingled roof, a lean-to bedroom, a large stone fireplace, dirt floors, and a commanding view of the lake and the mountains to the east. He kept a wide assortment of pistols, muskets, swords, and bayonets stacked against his fireplace, both for his own protection as well as for trading with the local Utes and the various hunting and fishing parties that occasionally visited the lake. Since his original homestead claim included Crawshaw's old cabin, Wescott left it standing for use as a guest house.

The summer of 1867 was by all accounts an idyllic time for Wescott, who spent his days hunting, fishing, and trapping to his heart's content. He played host for noted explorer and Civil War veteran John Wesley Powell, who arrived in the company of Wescott's old friend Jack Sumner. While leading his geological survey crew through Middle

Park, Powell had met Sumner in Hot Sulphur Springs, and together they journeyed to Grand Lake in order to visit Wescott. Powell thus became one of the first, and arguably the most famous, travelers to enjoy Joseph Wescott's renowned hospitality.

Like Crawshaw before him, Wescott had to endure the full fury of a Rocky Mountain winter alone. A young fisherman who had been staying with the Judge during the autumn of 1867 offered to haul their large catch of trout to Georgetown, where he would sell the fish and return with a supply of food to last the coming winter. Wescott agreed, then waited patiently as weeks passed with no sign of the young man. Soon the deep snows and arctic cold of winter set in. Fishing and hunting became extremely difficult. Wescott's meager food supply dwindled away to nothing, forcing him to resort to desperate measures in order to avoid starving to death. In *Ghosts of the Shootin'*, local historian Nell Pauly wrote that the starving Wescott "cut the deer hide from the seat of his chair and boiled it to a glutinous mixture, adding, for seasoning, a few herbs he was able to dig from the ground under the snow." The "demented and delirious" Wescott evidently ate his shoes in the same manner, and by the time spring finally arrived he was quite near death before a small hunting party miraculously stumbled upon his isolated cabin and saved his life. Only later did he learn that the young fisherman had sold all of the trout, as well as the burros used to haul them, and pocketed the money for himself. Undaunted, Wescott recovered and remained a fixture in Grand Lake until his death in 1914.

THE FIRST ASCENT OF LONGS PEAK

The summer after his ordeal, Joseph Wescott once again welcomed John Wesley Powell to Grand Lake. Powell arrived in August 1868 with an ambitious plan to lead the first climb of Longs Peak. Accompanying him were William Byers, editor of the *Rocky Mountain News,* Byers' brother-in-law Jack Sumner, Powell's younger brother Walter, and three of Powell's students. Byers had tried and failed to summit Longs Peak from the Estes Park side in 1864, prompting him to predict that the 14,255-foot mountain would never be climbed, despite persistent claims that Arapaho warriors routinely hid on the summit in an effort to trap eagles. When Powell offered him another opportunity to ascend the peak, Byers jumped at the chance to prove his earlier prediction wrong. The climb also provided Byers with an intriguing story for his *Rocky Mountain News*, and he dutifully filed dispatches on the progress of Powell's expedition as it journeyed from Hot Sulphur Springs up the Colorado (Grand) River to Grand Lake:

> Leaving the sage plain, we traveled over timbered ridges—the timber nearly all killed by fire and much of it fallen down—separated by beautiful, grassy, park-like valleys, and came again to the [Grand] river at Stillwater.... Here the two main forks of the river unite; the North Fork, which is much the longest stream, coming directly from the north.... Crossing another meadow, half a mile wide, we reach the main or Lake Fork, looking like a great lagoon, two hundred feet wide, and three feet deep, with scarce any current...and the water so clear that a pin could be distinguished on the bottom. A mile and a half further along a fringe of pines, across a meadow, through a belt of trees, a little sage opening, then another belt of pines, with a high mountain on the right [Shadow Mountain], and piles of boulders on the left, and we are at the margin of the lake.

The quest to summit Longs Peak began on the west shore of the lake near Wescott's cabin, where Byers noted in one of his dispatches that "about twenty-five people" were fishing from the shore. Powell is said to have bunked in Crawshaw's old cabin, and he and his crew enjoyed Wescott's company for a few days before packing out on August 20, loaded with "ten days' rations," although according to Byers they "expected to make the trip in much less time." Crossing the outlet, they bushwhacked their way along the north shore of the lake, "through a dense mass of brush and fallen timber, and at a point directly opposite our camp" began their ascent into the mountains. Their route took them past what is now known as Adams Falls, up the East Inlet towards Mount Craig (also known as Old Baldy or Roundtop), and finally to their first camp near timberline on the western slope of Mount McHenry, just below the crest of the Continental Divide.

The climbers wasted the next day trying to find their way around an "impassable precipice," then spent another cold night encamped near timberline. At first light they decided to leave their horses behind and continue on foot, but every route they attempted dead-ended with a dangerous, gaping chasm or a nearly-vertical slope of loose rock. Frustration compelled the group to abandon their plans and head for Wild Basin, where they camped about a quarter of a mile from Sandbeach Lake. The summit appeared much more attainable from this location, and one of Powell's students, L.W. Keplinger, took it upon himself to reconnoiter the route. He ascended to within about eight hundred feet of the top, then returned to camp well after dark. Byers described that night as a "most cheerless one, with gusts of wind and sprinkles of rain; our only shelter under the sides of an immense boulder, where we shivered the long hours through."

The next morning, August 23, 1868, dawned cold and clear. Following Keplinger's route, the climbers scrambled up the peak and by ten o'clock they were standing on the summit. Powell's ascent was especially remarkable, considering that he had lost his right arm to a Confederate bullet at the Battle of Shiloh in 1862. Finding absolutely no evidence of previous human activity on the summit, the climbers congratulated one another on their accomplishment. Someone (historian Wallace Stegner contends that "it could only have been Byers") produced a bottle of wine, and the hardy climbers toasted to their success. Byers noted in his journal that Denver was "plainly distinguishable to the naked eye; also the Hot Springs in the Middle Park," then joined his fellow climbers in constructing a small rock cairn topped by a flag. Inside the cairn they placed an old tin can that contained their names, the date, temperature and barometric readings, and other assorted memorabilia of their climb. After lingering on the summit for nearly three hours, the climbers began the treacherous descent, which they accomplished without incident. On August 24 they arrived back in Grand Lake after recovering their horses, thereby completing a remarkable five-day trip that culminated with the first recorded ascent of Longs Peak.

William Byers went on to great fame as an irrepressible booster for the future state of Colorado, and eventually his name graced both a canyon and a beautiful mountain in Middle Park. John Wesley Powell later received tremendous acclaim for leading the first scientific expedition down the entire Colorado River, accompanied by none other than Jack Sumner. As for Joseph Wescott, he continued to hunt and fish on the shores of his beloved Grand Lake, spinning tall tales for a steady stream of visitors that included at least one notorious mountain man and one soon-to-be famous photographer.

ROCKY MOUNTAIN JIM

Variously described as a talented hunter and trapper, a drunkard and a poet, a liar and a ruffian, a chivalrous gentleman and an all-around adventurer, the dashing and handsome James Nugent was well-known throughout the Colorado high country as Rocky Mountain Jim. Genuine facts concerning his past are scarce at best, but Nugent himself claimed that he was the son of either a southern general or a British army officer stationed in Canada. He bragged about working as a trapper for the Hudson's Bay

Company, and claimed to have fought with Quantrill's raiders (if true, perhaps it was Nugent who relieved Philip Crawshaw of his gold in 1861). Historic sources are unclear about the exact date, but sometime around 1868 Nugent staked his claim to 160 acres at the head of Muggins Gulch, near the entrance to the new settlement of Estes Park. Reports concerning his near-fatal encounter with an angry bear near Grand Lake are somewhat more reliable, although again, the exact date is in question.

Different versions of the story include a wide variety of details, but most agree that sometime during the summer of either 1868, 1869, or 1871, depending upon which historical source is consulted, Rocky Mountain Jim headed for Denver with his dog and a mule to sell a load of furs and partake of the town's many amenities. After what is described as a "riotous visit," Jim decided to return home via Middle Park and Grand Lake in order to do a little hunting. On July 6, while tracking some deer about eight miles south of Grand Lake, Jim was startled by the sight of his dog crashing through the underbrush, followed closely by a large female grizzly bear with her two cubs. The terrified hound ran straight for Jim, as did the enraged bear, and Jim realized to his dismay that he had left his rifle back at camp. Leveling his revolver, Jim squeezed off four shots before the beast was upon him, her massive jaws tearing through his left elbow. Jim shoved his revolver against the bear and fired his fifth shot; his sixth (and last) bullet misfired. Desperate now, he dropped the gun and began slashing wildly with his knife. The wounded bear released Jim's mangled arm, seized him by the head, and tore the scalp from the right side of his skull, an injury that caused Jim to lose consciousness.

Jim awoke sometime later and discovered to his astonishment that he had killed the bear, but the battle had cost him dearly; his left arm and nearly-severed left thumb hung limp and useless at his side, and a crimson flap of shredded scalp covered his right eye. Bleeding profusely, delirious with pain, Jim somehow managed to crawl back to his camp and climb aboard his mule. He then set off for a harrowing ride to Grand Lake. In Mary Cairns' version of the story, Jim's dog Ring raced off like Lassie to alert Judge Wescott in Grand Lake, who followed the dog back to the scene of the attack, rendered first aid, then hauled Jim on a makeshift stretcher back to his cabin.

Reaching the lake, Jim encountered two young Frenchman who were staying at Wescott's cabin. Fearful of Indian attack, the two men initially thought that Jim had been scalped. With Wescott's help they overcame their anxiety and bound his wounds as best they could, then sent for the nearest doctor. News of Jim's injuries eventually reached a mining camp about fifteen miles distant, where a Doctor Pollack happened to be tending the sick. The doctor rushed to Grand Lake and administered what little aid he could before leaving Jim in the capable hands of Joseph Wescott, who slowly nursed the wounded man back to health.

Over the course of his recovery, James Nugent and Joseph Wescott apparently formed a genuine friendship, a friendship that historian Caroline Bancroft contends was the first act of "hands across the divide," a symbolic representation of the strong historic connection between Grand Lake and Estes Park. Although the two towns strengthened their connection in later years, the friendship between the Judge and the mountain man proved to be short-lived. With Wescott's help, Jim recovered and returned to his homestead near Estes Park, where he soon became embroiled in disputes with his fellow settlers over competing land claims. After festering for months, the animosity erupted in gunfire. At least five different versions of the story have surfaced, each with its own particular details, but all of them agree that on June 19, 1874, a settler named Griff Evans leveled a shotgun at Rocky Mountain Jim and emptied both barrels. Jim lingered until September before succumbing to his wounds.

Photographs of Rocky Mountain Jim are decidedly scarce. A portrait of him by artist Ken Keith that appeared in Harold M. Dunning's history of Estes Park, *Over Hill and Vale*, suggests a strong resemblance to Errol Flynn. Isabella Bird, who visited Estes Park in 1873 and wrote about her adventures in *A Lady's Life in the Rocky Mountains,* described Jim's face as "remarkable," noting that he must have been "strikingly handsome" before the bear attack, but now "one eye was entirely gone, and the loss made one side of his face repulsive, while the other might have been modeled in marble."

Thanks in part to the romantic imagination and wonderfully descriptive letters of Isabella Bird, James Nugent became a legend in the Estes Park/Grand Lake region shortly after he met his untimely end. The legend continued to grow in subsequent years as an abundance of literary license and downright exaggeration so embellished his life that it became difficult to separate the fact from the fiction. Historic accounts of another famous visitor to Judge Wescott's home on the shores of Grand Lakes are much more reliable, primarily because for the first time in history the stories are supplemented with photographic evidence.

Perhaps the first photograph of Grand Lake, taken by William Henry Jackson during the summer of 1874. (Courtesy Colorado Historical Society)

FIRST PHOTOGRAPHS

Traveling under the auspices of Ferdinand Vandeveer Hayden's United States Geological and Geographical Survey of the Territories, renowned frontier landscape photographer William Henry Jackson arrived in Grand Lake on July 30, 1874, in the midst of a typical summer squall:

William Henry Jackson in 1872, age 29. The renowned frontier photographer took the first known photographs of Grand Lake in August 1874. (From Jackson, William Henry. Time Exposure: The Autobiography of William Henry Jackson. New York: G.P. Putnam's Sons, 1940)

We crossed the two forks [the North and Lake Forks of the Grand] within a short distance of each other. Just before we reached the first crossing a severe hailstorm came up, accompanied with intense lightning and deafening thunder—the hail pelted so hard that it annoyed our mules very much & they disliked exceedingly to face it. It was very cold and chilly & but for our rubbers and overcoats would have been very cold. We reached the Lake in a drenching shower, slung off the packs in double quick order and took refuge in the fisherman's hut until the worst of it was over...

A famous early image of Grand Lake, taken on the west shore by William Henry Jackson in August 1874. Titled "Fisherman's Cabin on Grand Lake," the image includes what may be Joseph Wescott's cabin. Note the elk antlers in the foreground, Craig Point at middle right, and what appears to be fire damage in the hazy distance. (Courtesy United States Geological Survey)

Presumably, the "fisherman's hut" where Jackson and his party sought shelter from the storm belonged to Joseph Wescott, although Jackson's journal never specifically mentions Wescott by name. Instead, he refers to the occupant of the cabin as simply "the Fisherman." Historian Caroline Bancroft wrote in 1968 that "Wescott was enormously interested in all of Jackson's equipment," and thought that the photographer was nuts for hauling it all over the mountainous West, yet Jackson's journal contains no evidence to support Bancroft's assertions. A meticulous record-keeper, Jackson did note that "a half dozen or so of men...have squatted and built cabins upon the shore," and that "a great many pleasure seekers find their way here," a clear indication of Grand Lake's early popularity as a tourist destination. He described the lake as "an irregular egg or pear shape, with two good size streams entering and a large outlet on the West," with water that was "clear limpid and cold, in the center a jet black."

1874 Jackson photo of Grand Lake looking north-northeast. The unusually murky water may be the result of inclement weather coupled with the extremely long exposures Jackson used to create his photographs.
(Courtesy United States Geological Survey)

As a writer, Jackson may have lacked the eloquence and audacity of William Byers, but he made no pretense about being a talented wordsmith. His true gift was photography, a skill that gained him considerable wealth and even greater acclaim. Among his many accolades, Jackson is widely credited with taking the first photographs of Grand Lake, including one well-known image titled "Fisherman's Cabin on Grand Lake." Whether or not the cabin in the photograph belonged to Joseph Wescott is difficult to determine; its architecture and relative location are consistent with historic descriptions of his cabin, but Jackson left few other clues in his journal. A close examination of the photograph does reveal elk antlers in the foreground, the spit of land known as Craig Point (named for Reverend Bayard Craig of Denver) protruding into the lake to the right, and what appears to be fire damage in the hazy distance.

Another Jackson photograph of the lake, taken from the south shore, is a view across some surprisingly murky water up the canyon of the North Inlet, with a tangled snag

31

1874 Jackson photo of Grand Lake looking west from the base of Baldy (Mt. Craig). The East Inlet meanders through stands of timber in the foreground, Grand Lake is barely visible in the middle distance, and the roiling thunderclouds above later drenched Jackson and his crew. The line across the photo is due to damage on the original negative. (Courtesy United States Geological Survey)

of downed timber in the foreground. The north shore, an area that is currently punctuated with an abundance of summer cabins, shows absolutely no signs of human activity. The murky water is a bit of a mystery, given the lake's reputation for crystal clarity, but it may be the result of the cloudy, rainy weather coupled with the extremely long exposures that Jackson used to create his photographs.

The inclement weather that plagued Jackson during his three-day visit evidently failed to dampen his enthusiasm for exploring the region around Grand Lake. His journal notes that he convinced "the Fisherman to get up his little king of a boat & take us over to a neighboring point," while a subsequent passage describes a journey across the lake and up the East Inlet towards Mount Craig:

It was a delightful ride, the early morning light shimmering over the surface of the deep dark waters of the lake, the low hanging wreathing clouds, clinging about the mountain peaks and the exhilarating air, made one feel all the enthusiasm such scenes inspire. Arrived on the far shore some little time ahead of the others, and as soon as they arrived put the packs in such shape as to divide the load equally....Took the north side of the cañon and started in.... The whole surface was entirely innocent of any travel, and fallen timber almost entirely barred our way.

Jackson and his companions bushwhacked up the inlet, then climbed the rocky north side of the valley to a point where they "took a good long look at the small snow spot on the summit of Round Top" (also known as Baldy or Mt. Craig, another honor for Reverend Bayard Craig). Jackson then set up his bulky box camera and captured the view looking back down the valley. The resulting image includes the East Inlet meandering through stands of timber in the foreground, Grand Lake faintly visible in the middle distance, and roiling thunderclouds moving in from the west, clouds that eventually soaked Jackson and his crew with a "lively hail and rain storm."

Beyond their obvious appeal as historic images of a pristine, undeveloped landscape, William Henry Jackson's 1874 photographs of Grand Lake mark the beginning of a new chapter in the region's history. Within a few short years after his visit, the discovery of rich mineral ores in the mountains near Grand Lake transformed Wescott's tiny, almost insignificant collection of crude cabins along the west shore of the lake into a genuine, full-blown frontier boom town on the north shore, complete with guest houses, grocery stores, sawmills, and saloons. Not surprisingly, the explosive growth coincided with the most tumultuous years in the entire history of Grand Lake, an era characterized by jealous rivalries, political intrigue, financial disasters, at least one cold-blooded murder and subsequent jailbreak, and a spectacular shootout that rivals the infamous Gunfight at the OK Corral. As has been the case throughout human history, however, the beginning of a new era necessarily required the ending of another.

CHAPTER FIVE

THE UTES MUST GO

The increasing numbers of settlers, hunters, and prospectors who filtered into Middle Park during the 1860s and 1870s did not go unnoticed by the Ute Indians. As early as 1862, local Indian Agents began hearing complaints from Utes who were angry about not receiving the gifts they had been promised. Tensions mounted when the Utes protested that it seemed as if the only Indians who ever received gifts from the U.S. government were those that killed settlers. Although no bloodshed ensued, the Utes did confront a small party of prospectors in Middle Park in June of 1863, stole their horses, and threatened violence unless the trespassers left the area. Later that summer, U.S. Army cavalry troops briefly entered Middle Park in response to sporadic Ute raids on the Overland Stage Line near Fort Hallack, Wyoming, but again, bloodshed was avoided. Subsequent negotiations kept things relatively peaceful for the next few years, and in 1868 the Utes agreed to a treaty that granted them exclusive ownership of the western third of Colorado, a treaty that was broken less than five years later after the discovery of new gold deposits in the San Juan Mountains. Hostilities resumed in Middle Park in 1870 when Utes burned down a blacksmith shop in Hot Sulphur Springs, followed by reports of a skirmish between Joseph Wescott and a small party of Arapaho Indians near Grand Lake. In 1872, gun-toting Utes forced a frightened resident to leave Hot Sulphur Springs. A year later, they burned down a building belonging to William Byers.

Despite their threats and posturing, the Utes continued to refrain from open warfare in Middle Park, prompting a Georgetown newspaper to report in August 1874 that they were "a bit more dangerous than lame, blind bears." This assessment proved somewhat premature. The creation of Grand County in early 1874 had given local settlers an official outlet for their complaints, and they responded in 1875 by petitioning for military protection from the Utes. The army dispatched a cavalry company to Hot Sulphur Springs, the new county seat, but by the time they arrived tensions had eased to the point that a permanent garrison was deemed unnecessary. Still, the situation continued to deteriorate. The discovery of rich mineral ores in the mountains near Grand Lake in 1875 inspired a small yet vig-

Rare photograph of a mounted Ute warrior in full-body war paint, accompanied by a small child. By 1880 the Utes had been forcibly removed from Middle Park to reservations in Utah and extreme southwestern Colorado. (Powell survey photo, no date, from Marsh, Charles S. People of the Shining Mountains. Boulder, CO.: Pruett Publishing Co., 1982)

orous rush of prospectors into the area, and Colorado's admission to the Union in 1876 virtually guaranteed even more settlement in the region. By 1877 another petition from settlers near Hot Sulphur Springs warned that "either we or the renegade Utes will be exterminated."

The situation finally exploded in early September, 1878, when a group of about forty Utes crested Berthoud Pass and began causing trouble near present-day Fraser, threatening residents, tearing down fences, and vandalizing farm equipment. Word of the disturbance quickly spread. Before long a posse from Hot Sulphur Springs arrived at the Ute encampment. In the ensuing altercation, prospector "Big Frank" Addison shot and fatally wounded a hot-headed Ute brave named Tabernash, very near where the present-day town of Tabernash is located. Miraculously, the conflict did not escalate as both sides cautiously moved off to reassess the situation. The Utes apparently buried their fallen comrade somewhere nearby, then followed the nervous posse as far as Hot Sulphur Springs. By morning the Utes had disappeared toward the west.

Shortly thereafter, on a ranch near present-day Kremmling, a small party of Utes bent on revenge for the murder of Tabernash put three bullets into the back of rancher Abraham Elliot. The incident aroused serious public indignation against the Utes, who responded with an indiscriminate and deliberate slaughter of game animals throughout Middle Park, including the last of the region's mountain bison. Demands for reprisals echoed across Colorado. Resentment was especially strong for one particularly disagreeable Ute leader known as Colorow. In the summer of 1879, incensed by broken promises and repeated treaty violations, Colorow devised a plan that he hoped would drive the white settlers from Indian lands forever, while at the same time drive desirable game animals toward Ute lands in western Colorado. He waited until favorable winds appeared, then instructed his followers to ignite the parched timber and dry grasses of the Colorado high country. The inferno spread quickly, destroying an estimated $10 million worth of timber and over 100,000 acres of grassland in North and Middle Parks, yet the settlers and prospectors refused to leave, as did the elk and bison and deer. The fires soon died out, and with them Colorow's plan to save his people. Vast stands of timber scorched by the fires can still be seen on the flanks of Jackstraw Mountain in Rocky Mountain National Park.

The final act of this tragic drama came during the autumn of 1879, when a party of Utes gunned down Indian

Agent Nathan Meeker and eleven of his employees near present-day Meeker, in western Colorado. Like the Arapahos before them, who by 1878 had been forcibly removed to reservations in Wyoming, Oklahoma, and Kansas, the Utes were forced at gunpoint to abandon their traditional lands and live on reservations in Utah and extreme southwestern Colorado. Although both the Utes and Arapahos left behind an abundance of Indian names and a few scattered, time-worn artifacts, little else beyond myths and legends remains to connect them to the lands that they had occupied for centuries.

The final removal of the Utes and Arapahos from Middle Park coincided with an era of profound change in Grand Lake. No longer threatened with Indian attack, increasing numbers of prospectors and miners poured into the region known as the Rabbit Ears Range, followed closely by the shrewd promoters and wily merchants eager to take advantage of the new arrivals. "Mining the miners," they called it, and their efforts initiated the cycle of boom and bust that characterized life in Grand Lake during the last decades of the nineteenth century.

CHAPTER SIX

ALL THAT GLITTERS

In July 1875 a pair of determined prospectors from Georgetown named Alexander Campbell and James H. Bourn discovered evidence of rich mineral ores in the rugged Rabbit Ears Range, about ten miles northwest of Grand Lake. Their strike eventually became known far and wide as the Wolverine Mine. Both the mountain looming high above the Wolverine and the gulch below it were promptly named for Jim Bourn, although a careless county clerk later misspelled his name "Bowen," an error that soon appeared on maps of the region. Ironically, Bowen Mountain is one of the two neighboring peaks that inspired early trappers to christen these mountains the Rabbit Ears Range in the first place, evidently because they resembled a rabbit's ears when viewed from Grand Lake. The other peak, Baker Mountain, took its name from Jack Baker, an early scout and trapper in the area. Modern travelers know these lofty mountains as the Never Summers, a shortened version of the original Arapaho name *Ni-chebe-chii* (Never-No-Summer), a reference to the snowfields that linger in these high peaks throughout the summer months.

Word of the Wolverine spread quickly throughout the Colorado high country. Before long a small swarm of prospectors arrived and began probing every peak, valley, gulch, and creek of the Rabbit Ears for any sign of mineral wealth. An ambitious miner named Joe Shipler arrived in 1876, built a log cabin along the North Fork of the Grand, and staked a promising silver claim on the flanks of what later became known as Shipler Mountain. Other prospectors joined Shipler in the quest for mineral riches, and new mines soon appeared with such names as the Hidden Treasure, the Wild Irishman, the North Star, the Ruby, and the Silent Friend. Despite the fact that crushing debt forced Campbell and Bourn to give up their claim to the Wolverine less than a year later, eager miners continued to pour into the area. Even the redoubtable Judge Wescott heard the loud echo of the mining boom. He, too, saddled up his trusty burro and set off prospecting.

LEGENDS OF GOLD, LININGS OF SILVER

Prior to the Rabbit Ears mining rush, the Grand Lake area had experienced only sporadic indications of mineral wealth. In fact, the best-known reference to mineral riches had absolutely nothing to do with the mines, but rather came from a legend of buried gold. It seems that sometime during the 1850s, a small party of prospectors returning East after striking it rich in the California Gold Rush was attacked by hostile Utes somewhere near present-day Steamboat Springs. The four miners who managed to escape with their lives made their way to Grand Lake, where they camped for several days and contemplated what to do with their fortune in gold dust. Frightened by the possibility of another attack, the miners decided to bury their treasure near the lake and return the following spring, armed with an arsenal of weapons in order to guard their precious cargo on the perilous journey across the Great Plains.

The miners emptied their loot into a Dutch oven (essentially a large covered pot) and buried it next to a rather substantial gray boulder shaped like a tombstone on the east shore of Grand Lake. One of the miners, dubious about ever locating the boulder again, took out his hunting knife and buried it up to the hilt in a nearby tree. Satisfied that the knife would help them locate the treasure, the miners resumed their journey home. They made it out of the mountains safely, but somewhere on the plains of eastern Colorado another Indian attack killed three of the miners. The lone survivor struggled home and lived long enough to tell his tale before succumbing to his wounds. Ever since, treasure hunters have searched for the hunting knife buried in the tree. Later versions of the legend claim that the treasure is still buried somewhere near the trail to Adams

Falls; others claim that extensive excavation work for the Colorado-Big Thompson Project in the early 1940s obliterated both the tree and the boulder. Either way, the treasure has never been located.

A different sort of buried treasure continued to attract miners to the Grand Lake area throughout the late 1870s and early 1880s. Although prospectors in the Rabbit Ears did discover some early indications of placer gold in the North Fork, they soon focused their attention and considerable energies instead on the region's apparently abundant supply of silver, copper, and lead-bearing ores. In June 1879 two Fort Collins promoters, William Baker and Benjamin Burnett, organized the Middle Park and Grand River Mining and Land Improvement Company for the sole purpose of establishing the town of Lulu City, about sixteen miles north of Grand Lake. Most historians agree that Lulu City, "The

The mining camp that later became Lulu City. The discovery of gold and silver along the North Fork of the Colorado River in the 1870s touched off a mining boom throughout the Rabbit Ears Range (Never Summer Mountains). According to historian Mary Lyons Cairns, the man at the extreme left is Ezra Kauffman, who later built a hotel in Grand Lake. Photo circa 1878. (Courtesy RMNPHC)

Coming Metropolis of Grand County," probably took its name from Benjamin Burnett's daughter Lulu ("the most beautiful girl I ever saw," according to Robert L. "Squeaky Bob" Wheeler, an early visitor who later developed a resort nearby), although it is possible that the name came from Lulu Stewart, daughter of a local mail carrier.

Located in the very midst of the mining excitement at an elevation of 9400 feet, Lulu City began as a small mining camp near the North Fork of the Grand (Colorado) River. Within a year a 160-acre town site had been surveyed and platted next to the river. An impressive array of businesses soon appeared, including a butcher shop, post office, real estate agency, two sawmills running day and night, a hotel, at least one saloon, a general store, and some forty cabins. "Blasts can be heard at any time of the day from mines [near] Lulu City," reported the Georgetown *Colorado Miner*. By 1881 several more businesses were up and running, including a clothing store, a barber shop, assorted hardware, grocery, and liquor stores, and a two-cabin red light district just north of town to service the region's miners. With stagecoaches arriving three times a week from Fort Collins and twice weekly from Grand Lake, Lulu City seemed poised for greatness.

Other mining camps along the North Fork soon followed suit. Dutchtown appeared high on the flanks of Lead Mountain, a handful of cabins founded by rowdy German exiles from Lulu City. Businessman Al Warner built a small cabin at the foot of Bowen (Bourn) Gulch, stocked it with groceries and booze, and began taking advantage of the considerable traffic heading to and from the Wolverine and other mines. Before long competitors moved in and opened their own stores, and in the process created the town of Gaskill, named for the Wolverine's first mining foreman, Lewis Gaskill. By 1882 Gaskill consisted of several buildings covering an area of almost sixty acres. Over on the west side of the Rabbit Ears, Teller City appeared with four saloons, a large hotel, and a population of nearly three

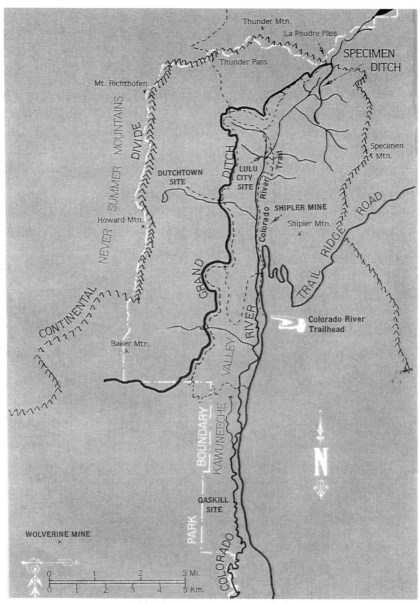

Rabbit Ears (Never Summer) - North Fork Mining District. (Courtesy RMNPHC

hundred. Early reports from the mines offered promises of "immense riches" for nearly anyone willing to stake a claim.

The astonishing growth of the boom towns on both sides of the Rabbit Ears created tremendous optimism in the region, yet the promise of prosperity was in fact an illusion. As early as 1876, United States Commissioner of Mining Statistics Rossiter Raymond had rated the prospects of the Rabbit Ears mines as "fair," a somewhat less than enthusiastic endorsement. His rating fell on deaf ears as miners and merchants alike either failed to recognize or couldn't bear to face a few important realities. First, the region's fierce winter weather severely hampered and occasionally halted both mining activities and transportation in the area. Second, the nearest ore processing smelters were at least sixty miles away, far too distant to insure profitable mining, and no one wanted to risk financing the construction of a smelter closer to the mines. Third, and perhaps most important of all, the mines of the Rabbit Ears consistently produced inferior, low-grade ores. Even when miners did manage to locate high-grade ores,

Photo looking north across the outlet, Craig Point in the middle distance. Note the fire damage and fish boxes along the shore, used to keep hooked fish alive. Photo circa 1879. (Courtesy Colorado Historical Society)

they had no choice but to pile it in great heaping mounds at mine entrances because there were no mills to process it. Virtually anyone paying attention or willing to face the facts should have plainly seen that these and other harsh realities would, within a decade, spell doom for the boom.

ECHOES DOWN VALLEY

Throughout the summer of 1875, as news of the Wolverine Mine initiated the rush into the Rabbit Ears, Judge Wescott continued his peaceful existence in Grand Lake, hosting a wide variety of hunters, fishermen, and tourists at his sleepy collection of cabins along the west shore. Two of his favorite visitors that summer were George and A. Phimister Proctor, the eldest sons of Denver businessman

Image printed in the 1881 edition of Crofutt's Grip-sack Guide of Colorado. *Compare with previous photograph.* (Courtesy Johnson Books, Boulder)

Alexander Proctor, who had given his boys permission to spend the summer hunting and fishing with the Judge. Under Wescott's tutelage they quickly became proficient outdoorsmen. Their skills and stories so impressed their father that in the summer of 1877, Alexander Proctor gathered his wife and eight children and headed for Grand Lake to build a cabin near Wescott's. The Proctors spent the next nine summers (and one winter) in Grand Lake, becoming the first non-native family to settle in the region on a semi-permanent basis.

A. Phimister Proctor ("Pheme" to his family; Wescott called him "Boss") went on to study art in New York and Paris, and eventually achieved great fame as an artist and sculptor. Two of his sculptures are currently located in Civic Center Park in Denver. His younger brother William became a respected Professor of Education at Stanford, while his sister Minnie is said to have inspired the title character in Patience Stapleton's novel *Kady*, which also includes a character named Judge West, evidently a thinly-veiled reference to Judge Wescott. The Proctors eventually stopped coming to Grand Lake, but they will always be recognized for their pioneering role in establishing and encouraging the practice of building summer cabins on the lake, a tradition that has continued ever since.

The fledgling community of Grand Lake, circa 1881. The mining boom of the late 1870s inspired rapid growth along the north shore of the lake. The large white structure near the center of the photo is Wilson Waldron's Grand Lake House hotel, where Waldron shot Robert Plummer in early 1883. (Courtesy RMNPHC)

Another view of Grand Lake looking toward the southwest, circa 1881. Note the foot bridge over the outlet in the middle distance and the scattered cabins along the west shore. (Courtesy Grand County Historical Association Museum)

Aside from being the Proctor's first summer, 1877 brought additional changes to Grand Lake. The first batch of official U.S. mail arrived in July, giving Judge Wescott, who had been appointed postmaster, the opportunity to carry out his duties with typical nonchalance. He simply set out an old canned-goods crate, tossed the mail inside, and stepped aside to allow folks to sort through it. Another development proved somewhat more problematic for the Judge. Over on the north shore of the lake, in a large level area not far from the North Inlet, several newcomers had built a few ramshackle cabins. This new construction deeply offended the Judge, who believed that his homestead on the west shore constituted the only legitimate settlement in Grand Lake. He even took to calling his side of the lake "Paradise," while he derisively referred to the settlement on the north shore as "Dublin." The east shore, where at least one cabin soon appeared, Wescott simply called "Hell Gate." He continued to promote the west side of the lake and sold portions of his homestead to summer visitors, but the broad sweep of flat land surrounding the new settlement virtually guaranteed that future commercial development would occur on the north shore. Within a year a sawmill and small store appeared, and when a Canadian-born entrepreneur named Wilson Waldron (also spelled Waldern) started construction on the Grand Lake House hotel in 1878, the site for the new town became a foregone conclusion.

Growth in Grand Lake closely coincided with the success of the mining boom in the Rabbit Ears. Its location at the southern end of the Kawuneeche Valley and (still primitive) road connections to the rest of Middle Park made it the perfect distribution point for supplies heading for the mines. As Lulu, Teller, and Gaskill prospered, so too did Grand Lake. The increase in traffic to the mines inspired Winslow and Lillian Nickerson to open the Grand Central Hotel and Restaurant in 1880, the town's second hotel. The east end of the Grand Central later became Grand Lake's first schoolhouse during the winter of 1881, with Wilson

Early visitors, probably miners, with their horses on the northwest shore of Grand Lake. Photo circa 1882. (Courtesy Grand County Historical Association Museum)

The Fairview House, Mary J. Young's hotel on the west shore near Craig Point. Built in 1881, the Fairview played a role in the infamous Fourth of July Shootout of 1883. Torn down in 1937. Photo circa 1883. (Courtesy Grand County Historical Association Museum)

The Garrison House, later called the Grandview Hotel. Built in 1881 on the west shore south of the outlet. The Grandview burned to the ground in 1901. Photo circa 1883. (Courtesy Denver Public Library, Western History Collection)

The view from the Grand Hotel, looking east. The boat in the photo is named the "Lake View." Photo taken by the rather appropriately named Harry Lake, circa 1900. (Courtesy Denver Public Library, Western History Collection)

Waldron's niece Miss McGee ("a very pretty young girl") serving as the first teacher. Mr. and Mrs. Henry Rhone bought the Grand Central in 1919 and turned it into the popular Corner Cupboard. The original building survived numerous alterations over the years, but was torn down in 2000 to make way for a new structure.

The year 1881 proved to be an auspicious time for the fledgling young community of Grand Lake. The town's basic layout finally took shape after a formal survey defined a town site consisting of forty-three blocks and a large public square. Plans for Grand Avenue, the town's main street, called for a one hundred-foot wide thoroughfare, large enough to accommodate rodeos, parades, horse and foot races, and other social events. A few of the false-front buildings so familiar in the frontier American West quickly appeared on both sides of the broad avenue, and although

Stagecoach of the Grand Lake Stage Line parked in front of James Cairns' first store, circa 1883. Cairns' store also served as the Grand Lake post office. Note the American flags in the store windows. According to Mary Cairns, the people sitting on the front seat of the stagecoach are Mr. and Mrs. Barney Day with their baby, Marian. Barney Day later met an untimely end in the Fourth of July Shootout of 1883. (Courtesy Grand County Historical Association Museum)

Wilson Waldron's Grand Lake House and a handful of other structures that had been completed prior to the survey did not exactly fit in with the master plan, most residents seemed quite pleased with the town's broad avenues and ample room for growth. Two more hotels, the Fairview House and the Garrison House (later known as the Grandview), soon graced the west shore of the lake.

Local residents helped erect the Fairview House at a good old-fashioned house-raising during the autumn of 1881 for a widow named Mary J. Young. Situated north of the outlet on Craig Point, the Fairview House boasted a commanding view of the lake and the surrounding mountains, and travelers came from miles around to admire the scenery and sample Mrs. Young's legendary cooking. The Fairview later gained notoriety for its role in the infamous Fourth of July Shootout of 1883 and continued as a Grand Lake landmark until 1937, when it was torn down to make way for new summer cabins.

Construction on the Garrison House began in the spring of 1881 on the west shore of the lake, south of the outlet. The view from the Garrison rivaled that of the Fairview, which almost certainly inspired Alex Adams to rename the hotel the Grandview when he bought it from original owner Tom Garrison (circa 1885?). Adams enlarged the hotel, added a second story, and refurnished the rooms with what local resident Josephine Young described as "the most beautiful furniture I ever saw." Sadly, fire consumed the entire structure in 1901.

James Cairns, a Canadian merchant who evidently saw great promise in the little town by the lake, constructed a general store on the corner of Grand Avenue and Pitkin Street shortly after the completion of the official townsite survey and platting in 1881. A solid citizen, Cairns proved

Interior of James Cairns' first store, circa late 1880s, well stocked with dry goods, canned goods, and bolts of fabric. In 1908 Cairns replaced this store with a larger structure. (Courtesy Grand County Historical Association Museum)

to be an "obliging and popular" businessman, offering easy credit and the occasional grubstake to various miners down on their luck. His store stocked all manner of merchandise and even served as the town post office, but Cairns is perhaps best remembered as the only merchant who continued operating his business after the collapse of the mining boom. He weathered the economic depression that followed, and in 1908 built a larger store to replace the first, which he operated until Matilda Humphrey bought the property in 1924. The remnants of Cairns' store still exist as part of the Humphrey Building. His wife, Mary Lyons Cairns, later wrote the definitive history of Grand Lake.

According to Mary Cairns, Grand Lake's first newspaper, the *Grand Lake Prospector*, also appeared in 1881, although historian Robert Black contends (quite convincingly) that the first issue actually came out in July 1882. Published by George W. Bailey and John Smart, the *Prospector* dutifully reported the local news until 1888, when economic depression and crippling debt forced Smart to lease the paper to Oscar Bryan, who moved the entire operation to Hot Sulphur Springs and changed the name to the *Grand County Prospector*, which eventually evolved into the *Middle Park Times*. George Bailey later became a judge for the Colorado Supreme Court, while Smart began editing for the *Denver Post*. The few surviving copies of the *Prospector* are highly valued by historians seeking information about Grand Lake's formative years.

Aside from being a time of explosive growth, 1881 is perhaps best remembered as the year that political maneuvering transferred the county seat from Hot Sulphur Springs to Grand Lake. Hot Sulphur had been the center of local government ever since the creation of Grand County in 1874, and it had served its function well. Its location near the center of the sprawling county had assured equal representation for ranchers and miners alike. Yet by 1880, certain elements in and around Grand Lake began arguing that Hot Sulphur was simply too far away to represent the growing populations of the eastern and northern portions of the county, specifically the boom towns along the North Fork and in North Park, and that Grand Lake would make a better location for the county seat.

Advocates on both sides of the issue filed and counter-filed petitions while bitterness and recriminations festered, and the question was eventually put to a vote on November 2, 1880. Grand Lake came out on top, 114 to 83, but representatives with strong ties to Hot Sulphur managed to overturn the vote on a technicality and declared the matter closed. The following April, however, a new Board of Commissioners with a decidedly pro-mining disposition reviewed the technicality and ruled in favor of Grand Lake. The Board then ordered that all official records and duties be transferred to Grand Lake, and shortly thereafter awarded a construction contract for a new courthouse and jail to builder Tom Johnston. Within forty-eight hours the new building stood on Grand Avenue across the street from James Cairns' store.

Supporters of Hot Sulphur's claim to the county seat vehemently protested the decision, and eventually argued their case all the way to the Colorado Supreme Court, which sent the case back to the District Court. There, on August 18, 1882, Judge Chester Carpenter finally ruled in favor of Grand Lake, which presumably settled the matter. It didn't, of course, and within a year the dispute would force desperate men to settle their differences with bullets and blood.

CHAPTER SEVEN

A TURN FOR THE WORSE

Grand Lake had enjoyed a truly banner year in 1881, but murder and mayhem characterized the years that followed as an astonishing series of tragedies descended upon the little town, starting with the untimely death of a popular local citizen. Jules C. Harmon had arrived in Middle Park with his brother in 1878; a year later, he had been appointed postmaster of Hot Sulphur Springs, Deputy County Assessor, and Clerk of the District Court. In addition, Harmon served ably as the superintendent of the Hidden Treasure mine in Bowen Gulch, a job that unfortunately ended up costing him his life.

Concerned about the safety of his men, Jules Harmon left the bunkhouse at the Hidden Treasure mine on the morning of December 14, 1882, with plans to break a new trail to the mine entrance. He considered the old trail to be too steep and exposed, and shortly after he stepped outside his worst fears became a deadly reality. Without warning, an enormous avalanche broke loose from the slopes above the mine and swept Harmon six hundred feet down the mountain, burying him under a crushing cascade of snow and debris. Upon hearing the deafening roar of the deadly slide, Harmon's brother Everett and several other miners rushed to the scene and frantically searched for signs of life. Hours later they abandoned their efforts, leaving Harmon's body encased in its icy tomb until the following summer.

On December 23 a solemn obituary in the *Prospector* lamented the fact that the size of the slide made it "utterly impossible for poor humanity to do aught but wait until the bright sun of spring shall dissolve the beautiful but pitiless shroud which now envelops him, and give back to his family all that is mortal of this truly noble man." Ironically, that same edition of the *Prospector* also carried an announcement for an event that figured prominently in Grand Lake's next major tragedy: "The invitations for the New Year's Ball at the Grand Lake House have been issued. A large attendance is looked for, and an enjoyable time anticipated." In the aftermath of Jules Harmon's tragic death, the somber citizens of Grand Lake welcomed news of the gala event, and Wilson Waldron's Grand Lake House seemed the perfect place for such a party. The large building had many rooms with "Spring Beds, Mattresses, and Everything", and included a dining room that could seat seventy-five people, more than adequate to contain the expected crowds.

Waldron and his wife Eleanor had settled in Grand Lake in 1878. Two years later Eleanor gave birth to a son, Roy, who gained distinction for being the first white child born in the area. Their hotel and other financial investments (including interest in at least one local mining company) prospered, and Waldron's friendly disposition and political acumen eventually inspired local citizens to elect him county commissioner. He shrewdly used his office to promote Middle Park in general and Grand Lake in particular, especially the amenities of his fine hotel. Yet Waldron also earned a reputation for having a nasty temper; he once mercilessly beat a man during a dispute over which side of the lake would be better suited for the new town site. Folks in Grand Lake soon learned just how violent Waldron's temper could be.

The written historical record is unclear about exactly when the tragedy at the Grand Lake House occurred. Mary Lyons Cairns claims it happened the night of December 31, 1882; Robert Black contends it took place at ten a.m. on January 2, 1883, but all versions of the story agree that wild dancing, fine food, and strong drink fueled the festivities as the New Year's Ball got underway. Despite the deep snow, a great many local citizens, ranchers, and miners arrived at the hotel to join in the revelry. Wilson Waldron in particular seems to have enjoyed himself by consuming a prodigious quantity of alcohol. At some point during the party, Waldron encountered his wife sitting in a rocking chair nursing their youngest child. In a drunken stupor he began teasing the baby. Annoyed and perhaps a little frightened, Eleanor Waldron discretely asked a young miner named Robert Plummer to escort her husband from the room. Plummer tried gentle persuasion at first, then resorted to physical force. Predictably, the situation quickly spiraled out of control. Plummer's actions absolutely infuriated the drunken Waldron, who staggered over and removed his rifle from a rack on a nearby wall. Seeing this, Plummer prudently made his way to the exit. Just as he entered a small log building across the street, Waldron put a bullet through his back and killed him.

The real Wild West. Mounted riders in front of the Grand Lake Saloon, circa 1883. (Courtesy RMNPHC)

Deputies promptly arrested Waldron and locked him up in the new jailhouse. Despite rumors of a lynch mob, he enjoyed a remarkable degree of freedom. A friendly jailer, who apparently did not understand his job description, allowed Waldron to take walks around town while awaiting his trial date. When turmoil in the county forced the postponement of the trial from August until October,

Waldron decided to escape. On the evening of September 14, 1883, the hapless jailer arrived with Waldron's dinner, and instead of sliding it through the slot in the door as he usually did, he simply walked into the cell. Seizing his opportunity, Waldron attacked the jailer and knocked him unconscious, then disappeared into the night. The local sheriff made a half-hearted attempt to locate the fugitive but soon abandoned his efforts to concentrate on his bid for reelection. A story in the *North Park Miner* later complained about the "barbarity displayed by the said Waldron against the jailer, a harmless fellow, who had treated Waldron like a prince, and allowed him to go just about where he wanted to."

After Waldron's escape his wife took their five young children and relocated to Golden, leaving behind a hotel full of furniture. Various eyewitnesses reported seeing Waldron in Teller City shortly thereafter, and Everett Harmon, brother of Jules, claimed that he had seen Waldron near Cripple Creek. Despite these and other sightings, Waldron managed to elude capture and is said to have died some years later. His Grand Lake House remained unoccupied until September 1884, when Mrs. Walker McQuery purchased all of the furniture and moved it to Hot Sulphur Springs. The once elegant building fell into a state of shocking disrepair, plagued by rumors of malevolent ghosts haunting its hallways, apparently angry over the lack of justice for Robert Plummer. New owners finally tore the old hotel down in 1923 to make way for the Pine Cone Inn.

In February 1883, barely two months after the murder of Robert Plummer, tragedy struck yet again. A large snowslide slammed into a cabin at the Toponis mine in Bowen Gulch, killing three miners and raising the winter's death toll to five. These latest deaths came as a considerable shock to local residents still reeling from Plummer's murder, who surely must have felt as if a curse had descended upon them. Mercifully, the spring thaw eventually eased winter's icy grip and brought a welcome respite from the threat of deadly avalanches. High mountain passes hopelessly clogged with snow began opening, miners who had chosen to winter in warmer climes began trickling back into the Rabbit Ears, and soon the sultry winds of early summer brought the season's first tourists, along with a resumption of regular mail service. In spite of the recent tragedies, Grand Lake's future looked promising indeed. Yet a bitter dispute still festered among certain corrupt and ambitious citizens, a dispute that would eventually lead to an even greater tragedy for the little town on the shores of the beautiful mountain lake.

BLOOD ON THE SHORE

Much has been written about the infamous shootout that occurred on the shores of Grand Lake on July 4, 1883. The details of the deadly altercation (best described in Black's *Island in the Rockies)* are complex, a tangled web of intrigue steeped in petty jealousies, personal rivalries, and political subterfuge involving some of the most prominent and powerful men in Grand County. The principal characters in the drama can essentially be divided into two rival factions. One faction included Chicago lawyer E.P. Weber, partner in the newly formed Grand Lake Mining and Smelting Company, superintendent of the Wolverine Mine, and Grand County Commissioner; Thomas J. "Cap" Dean, resident of Hot Sulphur Springs, saloon owner, and Clerk of the County Court; and Judd "Barney" Day, longtime rancher and also a Grand County Commissioner. In the other faction, Chicago lawyer John G. Mills, Teller City resident and Chairman of the Grand County Commissioners; Charles Royer, Sheriff of Grand County; and William Redman, Deputy Sheriff of Grand County.

The two Chicago lawyers, Weber and Mills, had arrived in Grand County at roughly the same time to represent the interests of shareholders who had invested in the mines along the North Fork. Both ambitious Republicans, the two had been friends but eventually had a falling out over local politics. They later clashed over who should represent Grand

County at the Republican state convention. During a shouting match in the middle of a Denver street, Mills threatened Weber with a "real showdown" once they returned to Grand County. Animosity also existed between Weber and Deputy Redman, primarily because Weber had spoiled a mine sale that would have netted $4000 for Redman. Other contentious issues, such as the transfer of the county seat from Hot Sulphur to Grand Lake, the lack of representation for North and Middle Park ranchers (represented by Mills), and a confusing series of tax and libel disputes all contributed to the hostilities brewing between the two rival camps.

Once again, the historical record is rife with discrepancies concerning exactly what happened, but all versions of the story agree that the morning of July 4, 1883, dawned clear and calm, with barely a ripple disturbing the still waters of Grand Lake. Weber, Day, and Dean convened at the Fairview House for a leisurely breakfast, then lingered for a while enjoying the beautiful view and discussing the relative merits of local resident Jake Pettingell's new fishing rod. Sometime after eight o'clock the three men left the Fairview and headed west along the lake shore towards town, where they planned to attend a commissioner's meeting at the courthouse. The only disturbance came from firecrackers and an occasional gunshot echoing across the lake in anticipation of the big Fourth of July celebration planned for later that day. Eyewitnesses reported that the men seemed completely at ease as they walked away from the Fairview, although both Day and Dean were packing loaded .45-caliber pistols. Weber, apparently unarmed, carried only a bundle of papers.

Unbeknownst to the trio, a group of three masked men (some reports say four or more, possibly including William Redman's brother Mann and the Coffin brothers) had taken up positions behind a jumbled pile of large, glacial boulders along the shore, their horses tethered in a copse of lodgepole pines nearby. One of the men carried a .40-caliber Sharps rifle, and just as Weber and his companions reached the old log structure known as the Anderson cabin (which served as the Fairview's icehouse) the rifleman fired, striking Weber in the chest. Startled, Day and Dean turned to assist him when the masked ambushers emerged and opened fire. Dean drew his pistol and leveled it before a bullet tore through the bridge of his nose, sending him spinning in a shower of blood. Another bullet struck him in the right hip, shattering his thigh bone. He was then beaten about the head with the butt of a revolver. Day managed to squeeze off four shots; one bullet hit the rifleman square in the face, while another staggered the attacker next to him. Day then caught a bullet that sent him reeling into the lake. The surviving gunmen left their fallen comrade face down on the trail and quickly retreated, leaving Weber and Dean barely conscious and bleeding profusely, while Day's lifeless, half-submerged body bobbed gently in the placid lake. A bullet had shredded his heart, killing him instantly.

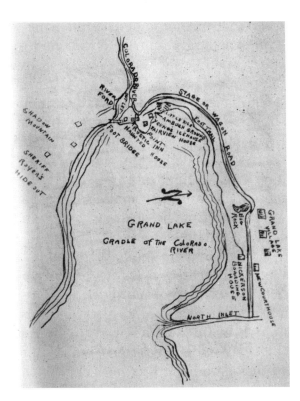

Map of Grand Lake showing relative location of the "ambush ground" and various structures associated with the Fourth of July Shooting of 1883. Note "Sheriff Royer's Hideout" to the left. (Courtesy Grand County Historical Association Museum)

At first the handful of folks milling around the Fairview thought the sound of gunfire coming from the lake shore had something to do with the celebration. One of them, Harry Snyder, decided to investigate and quickly alerted the others. Deputy Sheriff Max James from Teller City happened to be at the Fairview and quickly took charge of the scene. While the others tended to Weber and Dean, Deputy James walked to the body of the masked rifleman, turned it over, and tore off the disguise to reveal John G. Mills, dead from a gunshot wound to the head. He then gathered evidence from the scene and followed a trail of footprints and blood to some nearby trees, where it appeared as if a wounded man had been helped aboard a horse.

Back at the site of the ambush, bystanders assisted Cap Dean to his feet and helped him walk towards the Fairview, while the badly injured Weber had to be carried. News of the tragedy reached a Dr. H.F. Frisius of Teller, who happened to be in Gaskill at the time, but he arrived too late to save Weber; the mortally wounded commissioner soon slipped into a coma and bled to death on a cot in the Fairview. Dean had better luck. The bullet that had struck him in the nose was still lodged in the back of his skull, but seemed to have missed his brain completely. In fact, Dean appeared quite lucid, and even managed to provide a deposition with vital details of the shooting before an infection set in and claimed his life on July 17, 1883.

Curiously, no one had been able to locate either Grand County Sheriff Charles Royer or Deputy William Redman in the aftermath of the shooting. Royer had been scheduled for duty in Grand Lake that morning, but at noon on the Fourth of July he showed up in Hot Sulphur riding an obviously exhausted horse, which understandably aroused suspicions among local citizens. With no evidence against him, however, Royer kept his job as sheriff and launched a rather casual investigation into the shooting, which of course led nowhere. Royer soon left Grand County and reappeared in Georgetown, where he is said to have admitted his role in the shooting to a man named Adam Kinney. Royer's deepest anguish apparently came from shooting his old friend Barney Day

The site of the shooting, 1997. (Author photo)

through the heart. The two had remained close friends despite the animosity between their rival factions, and many suspect that Royer felt such tremendous guilt over killing Day that he committed suicide in a Georgetown hotel room on July 16. The gruesome death toll from the shooting now stood at five men: the Grand County sheriff, all three Grand County Commissioners, and the Grand County Clerk.

As for William Redman, he turned out to be the wounded gunman who fled the scene on horseback. He also vanished from Grand County, but later that summer a pair of cowboys rounding up stray cattle found his body in Utah, about four miles from the Colorado border. A subsequent investigation ruled that Redman had committed suicide, yet rumors persisted that he had been murdered in retaliation for his role in the Grand Lake shooting. Despite other rumors of Redman faking his death and escaping to Arizona (or New Mexico or Wyoming), evidence suggests that he did in fact die in Utah. Most histories therefore include his name in the list of victims from the Fourth of July tragedy, raising the death toll from the shootout to six men.

Sometime later Adam Kinney, the man who allegedly heard Sheriff Royer's confession in Georgetown, revealed what he knew about the shooting to Frank S. Byers (son of

William Byers). According to Byers, Kinney claimed that Royer had told him of a plot by Mills, Redman, and the Coffin brothers (one of whom, Alonzo, was the county jailer) to put a little scare into Weber, a scare that would convince him to leave the county for good. The "scare" clearly got out of hand, and Mills ended up shooting Weber, Redman shot Dean, and Day shot both Mills and Redman. Royer then shot his old friend Day through the heart and later committed suicide, as did William Redman. A tangled web indeed, and one that had profound repercussions for Grand Lake.

AFTERMATH

Newspapers across the region universally deplored the Grand Lake shooting, and summer businesses that catered to tourists noticed an immediate and significant reduction in their revenues. The little town (and the entire county, for that matter) had earned a reputation for lawlessness. The blatant escape of Wilson Waldron later that year certainly didn't help matters, and local businesses took another economic hit when hunters and trappers, fearing deadly avalanches as well as masked bandits, began avoiding the Rabbit Ears region altogether. The subsequent lack of revenue badly hurt Grand Lake merchants, but an even worse situation threatened to collapse the local economy entirely. The mines along the North Fork, which had once appeared so promising, had completely failed to live up to expectations.

The first indications of trouble came in April, 1883, when the famed Wolverine Mine temporarily shut down and laid off its entire work force. Lame explanations followed, including a dubious claim by the owners of the mine that they were simply trying to obtain more property before building a badly needed smelter. Smaller mines tried to hang on, but the winter of 1883 forced mine closures up and down the North Fork. Lulu City had been losing businesses and miners since at least the summer of 1882; when the post office shut down for the winter in November 1883 and residents began abandoning their homes and businesses, "The Coming Metropolis of Grand County" was already well on its way to becoming a ghost town.

Lulu City, July 1889. In ten years Lulu had gone from the "Coming Metropolis of Grand County" to a ghost town comprised of crumbling buildings and broken dreams, thanks to the failure of the North Fork mines. (Courtesy RMNPHC)

Teller City, Dutchtown, and Gaskill managed to hold out a little longer. As late as the summer of 1884, Teller reported a population nearing three hundred. By December 1885, it had lost its post office and most of its citizens. Although Gaskill's population never rose much higher than fifty, its residents had faith that the long-promised smelter would save their town. The smelter never materialized, and before long Gaskill consisted of little more than abandoned buildings and shattered dreams. Because of its location near timberline high above Lulu, Dutchtown probably never had a chance of becoming a real town anyway. It, too, became a ghost town, and by late 1886 virtually all mining in the Rabbit Ears Range had ceased.

Grand Lake resident Isaac Alden typified the hard-luck miners who toiled for years in hopes of striking it rich, at least until the mining crash delivered a sobering dose of reality. Alden, who claimed to be a direct descendant of John Alden of the storied Mayflower, first arrived in Grand Lake in 1880 and spent the next several years seeking his fortune. He apparently came very close one day while prospecting in the Soda Creek region southwest of Grand Lake, where he discovered indications of promising ore deposits. Alden carefully noted several landmarks in the area, including a large boulder and an enormous, uprooted pine tree, then set off to have the ore assayed.

Alden waited patiently while chemists in Denver analyzed his specimens. Finally, nearly a month later, news arrived that the specimens had indeed contained gold, at the considerable quantity of $1600 to the ton! Elated, Alden rushed back to his secret site to stake a claim, only to discover a barren, desolate landscape. A large forest fire had scorched the entire region during his absence, obliterating every trace of the uprooted tree and obscuring the large boulder under heaping piles of ash and debris. Alden spent the rest of his life searching for his lost treasure, and though he lived to the ripe old age of ninety, he never found it.

With the mining boom all but over, the town of Grand Lake struggled to survive. A few hardy residents remained, most notably James Cairns, who somehow managed to keep his general store open despite the lack of business. Cairns supplemented his meager income by homesteading a ranch, where he grew hay and tended a small herd of cattle. He also trapped bears and sold the enormous skins for a small profit. Other residents likewise found ways to survive, including Judge Wescott, who had spent the winter of 1884-85 in Aspen seeking silver but returned to resume his life of fishing, hunting, and spinning tall tales.

A final blow to Grand Lake's fortunes came in 1888, when Hot Sulphur Springs successfully regained the county seat. The move actually made considerable sense; the collapse of the mining boom had removed the primary

Freight wagon and buggy in front of James Cairns' store. Cairns kept his store open despite the mining failure, the only merchant in Grand Lake to do so. Photo circa 1896. (RMNPHC)

motivation for moving the county seat to Grand Lake in the first place, and the growth of ranching elsewhere in Middle Park created the need for a more centralized location for the county offices. Judge Wescott responded by platting what he called "Grand Lake City," a new town that he planned to carve from his original homestead on the west shore of the lake, just south the outlet. Wescott's dreams failed to materialize, as did long-anticipated plans for a railroad spur to Grand Lake. With the loss of the county seat and the payroll that went along with it, and no prospects for rail service, the little town that had endured so much tragedy and turmoil seemed destined to join the ghost towns along the North Fork, were it not for one crucial difference: the town's location on the shores of the beautiful mountain lake that had been attracting humans for over ten thousand years.

CHAPTER EIGHT

RESURRECTION AND RECOVERY

Unlike the ghost towns of the North Fork, Grand Lake never depended solely upon mining for its survival. The collapse of the mining industry in the Rabbit Ears severely damaged its economy, but Grand Lake already had a firmly established tourist infrastructure to fall back on; Lulu, Teller, and Gaskill did not. Survival proved difficult during the lean years following the failure of the mines, but eventually the tourists began returning. As always, the principal attraction was the lake, which remained popular with hunters, fishermen, and travelers in spite of the fear generated by the Fourth of July shooting and the economic turmoil created by the mining bust.

In a macabre sort of way, the shooting actually increased knowledge of Grand Lake throughout the state, as historian Robert Black noted in his definitive history of Middle Park, *Island in the Rockies.* Black quoted from an article in the Gunnison *Review-Press* which, somewhat incredibly, suggested that the whole episode had been a publicity stunt. "Until this week," the newspaper declared, "scarcely one in ten of the people of the State could tell where this [Grand] county was, or one in a thousand its county seat. The wholesale killing...brings it boldly to the front." Despite its hyperbolic accusation, the article did contain some small measure of truth: awareness of Grand Lake increased markedly throughout Colorado in the aftermath of the shooting. Furthermore, as memories of the tragedy began to fade during the last decade of the nineteenth century, the number of tourists visiting Grand Lake rose sharply, and some of those tourists ended up opening businesses and building summer cabins.

Because the railroads never reached Grand Lake, the establishment of dependable roads across the nearby mountains played a crucial role in the town's survival during the lean years, and in fact proved essential to the eventual development of the town's tourist-based economy. Miners hauling supplies from the Front Range (via Estes Park) to the mines along the North Fork utilized a variety of trails, but two of the most heavily-traveled routes followed old Indian trails. The first, which the Arapahos called the Dog's Trail (*ethebaw*) because its deep, lingering snow allowed dogs to pull sleds (or *travois*) over the mountains, later became the route of the scenic Fall River Road, the first automobile link between Estes Park and Grand Lake and an early tourist attraction in the area.

The second Indian trail was the standard route for miners traveling to the North Fork mines from Estes Park. The Arapahos called it the Child's Trail (*taieonbaa*), allegedly because sections of it were so steep that children often had to dismount and walk. Another explanation for the name comes from the early French-Canadian trappers in the region who called the Ute Indians "la tribe des Enfants" (Tribe of the Children), apparently because the Utes were, on the whole, a rather diminutive people, not much taller than children. The trail frequented by the Utes thus became the Child's Trail. Miners variously called this route the North Fork Trail, the Specimen Mountain Trail, Squeaky Bob's Trail, or the Poudre Lake Trail, but by 1915 the trail had officially been renamed the Ute Trail, its current designation. Parts of the Ute Trail closely parallel the present-day Trail Ridge Road, the highest continuous paved road in the United States and a route traveled by literally millions of tourists every year.

Despite heavy use by Indians and miners, neither the Dog's Trail or the Ute Trail (nor their successors, Fall River and Trail Ridge roads) ever carried as much traffic as Berthoud Pass, which became the principal corridor for travelers, mail, and freight heading to Grand Lake from Georgetown, Denver, and points east. A feasible route over Berthoud had been located as early as 1861, but only after completion of a durable road in 1874 did stagecoaches and freight wagons begin cresting the pass. This route proved especially important to the future of Grand Lake because it provided relatively convenient access for the increasing numbers of Eastern and Midwest tourists, as well as wealthy Denver residents, who began spending their summers at the lake during the late 1880s.

A great many of these early tourists came to Grand Lake seeking relief from the oppressive summer heat of eastern Colorado. Some simply camped in tents erected along the shores of Grand Lake; others stayed in the Grandview, the Fairview, or one of Judge Wescott's cabins. Soon, however, more and more families began building their own summer cottages and cabins at the lake, thereby continuing a tradition started by the Proctors in 1877. According to historian Mary Lyons Cairns, the first of these summer homes appeared in 1878, built by John Barbee (who later helped Joseph Wescott pen *The Legend of Grand Lake*) and William J. "Antelope Jack" Warren, an itinerant miner and early pioneer in the area. The Proctor family spent the winter of 1878-79 in the upstairs portion of this cabin.

Another early cabin appeared on a large rock on the south shore of the lake in 1889, constructed by Jay E. Adams. Adams sold the structure two years later, then built another, larger cabin near the East Inlet. Before Adams built this cabin, local residents referred to the scenic waterfall nearby as Ouzel (or Ousel) Falls, but sometime around 1907 the name was changed to Adams Falls in honor of Jay Adams. Other cabins (many described in considerable detail by Mary Lyons Cairns) began dotting the entire lakeshore during the late 1880s and early 1890s, followed by new businesses that catered to the summer tourists attracted by the lake's excellent hunting, fishing, and boating opportunities. By the turn of the century, Grand Lake had firmly committed itself to the burgeoning tourist trade.

The Kauffman House, a hotel constructed by early miner Ezra Hartzler Kauffman, appeared in 1892. Kauffman had arrived in Middle Park in 1877; in 1879 he guided one of the first groups of miners to a camp along the North Fork that later became the boom town of Lulu City. When the mines went belly-up, K a u f f m a n married Clara Johnston and moved to Hot Sulphur, where Clara gave birth to their two children, Mary and Carl. The K a u f f m a n s

The Kauffman House, a hotel built by Ezra Kauffman in 1892, one of the few surviving structures from Grand Lake's pioneer era. Listed on the National Register of Historic Places. (Courtesy Aron Rhone)

moved to Grand Lake in 1892 and stayed in Waldron's old Grand Lake House during construction of their new hotel. By 1899 Kauffman's wife had soured on frontier living and left with their children. Kauffman remarried in 1907, had three more children, and operated his hotel until his death in 1920. The building, which still stands near the center of town on the north shore of the lake, is listed in the National Register of Historic Places and houses a fascinating museum.

Christian Young, son of Fairview House owner Mary Young, built the Rustic Hotel with his wife Josephine on the west shore near the outlet in 1900. Mr. Young also operated a stage line that carried mail and passengers between Georgetown and Grand Lake three times a week. Like the Fairview, the Rustic witnessed its share of bloodshed. During a Saturday night dance in the hotel's large boathouse, an altercation erupted that resulted in the stabbing death of one of the revelers. Josephine Young remembered having to scrub bloodstains from the floor before Sunday School convened in the boathouse the next morning.

Mounted riders share a chuckle on the southwest shore, with the Grandview Hotel in the background. By the early 1890s Grand Lake began to recover from the collapse of the mining boom. 1898 photo. (Courtesy Denver Public Library, Western History Collection)

Preston H. Smith, who first came to Grand Lake in 1886, built the Hotel Bellevue on Grand Avenue in 1902. Smith operated the "largest and most pretentious" hotel in town (according to Mary Cairns) until the Bellevue burned down in 1912. Despite its brief existence, the success of the Hotel Bellevue helped confirm that tourism held the key to Grand Lake's economic future.

LIQUID TREASURE

The years following the mining bust also witnessed a renewed attempt to extract riches from the Rabbit Ears region, but this time it had nothing to do with gold or silver. The search for dependable water supplies fueled this new rush, and eventually led to the construction of what became known as the Grand Ditch (also known as the North Fork Ditch or the Grand River Ditch). Elegant in its simplicity, the plan for the Grand Ditch called for water from melting snow to be captured in a series of ditches angled toward La Poudre Pass (elevation 10,175 feet), where the water would be emptied into Long Draw Creek (by 1923 this became Long Draw Reservoir). From there the water flowed into the Cache La Poudre River, then down Poudre Canyon to the thirsty farms of Fort Collins and Greeley.

Initial excavations for the project began in 1881; by 1890 the six-foot deep, twenty-foot wide ditch began diverting water from the mountains above the North Fork to farmers and ranchers in eastern Colorado. Dug with picks and shovels by Swedish and Chinese laborers (historian C.W. Buchholtz also credits Japanese workers), the Grand Ditch grew longer as the demand for water increased. By 1932, the ditch stretched fourteen miles from Baker Gulch to La Poudre Pass. Current Grand Lake residents and travelers passing through Rocky Mountain National Park recognize the ditch as a tawny brown scar slashing its way across the eastern flanks of the Never Summer Mountains.

ANOTHER RACE FOR SILVER

Despite Joseph Wescott's haunting legend of fierce squalls and overturned rafts, boating had always been one of the most popular diversions enjoyed by early residents and visitors to Grand Lake. Wescott himself was an avid boater, and William Henry Jackson described taking a "delightful ride" across the lake during his visit in 1874. Rowboats and gaff-rigged (also known as square- or lateen-rigged) sailboats showed up in quite a few early photographs of the lake, many taken by Louis Charles McClure and the rather appropriately named Harry H. Lake. Docks appeared on the lake almost simultaneously with the earliest cabins, and before long summer residents began holding boat parades and carnivals. Not surprisingly, this early infatuation with boating soon led to the first official race, a contest between William Henry Bryant, a Denver attorney, and Richard Crawford Campbell, former newspaperman, prominent business manager, and son-in-law of Colorado

Boaters at the east end of the lake, circa 1892. Always a popular pastime on Grand Lake, boating enjoyed a surge in popularity with the creation of the Grand Lake Yacht Club in 1902. (Courtesy Colorado Historical Society)

Decorated boats wait in the North Inlet for a boat parade to begin, 1894. (Courtesy Dorothy O'Ryan.)

Senator Thomas Patterson. Bryant competed in a flat-bottomed scow, while Campbell chose a rowboat; both vessels were rigged with crude sails.

The outcome of that particular race remains in good-natured dispute, but in 1901 Bryant and Campbell, along with another Grand Lake summer resident,

A gaff-rigged (also known as a square- or lateen-rigged) sail transformed an early rowboat into a sailboat. Note the dog sitting with his master at the helm. Photo circa 1898. (Courtesy Denver Public Library, Western History Collection)

Fermor Spencer, conceived an audacious plan to form a yacht club. A year later they officially incorporated the Grand Lake Yacht Club, claiming the title of the highest registered yacht anchorage in the world (8,369 feet). Club members also registered an official "burgee" (a small, swallow-tailed pennant featuring the letters "GL" intertwined in red on a white background), established a hierarchy of officers and committees, and chose William Henry Bryant to serve as the Club's first Commodore.

Interest in the yacht club and its races grew with each passing year, increasing the demand for boats. With no rail service to Grand Lake (or Granby, until 1905), new sailboats had to be hauled over Berthoud Pass by freight wagon. These vessels gradually replaced the venerable old rowboats used by the lake's earliest sailors. Races were competitive but not cutthroat, and Dorothy O'Ryan, Bryant's granddaughter, fondly remembered the early days when standard sailing

William Henry Bryant, the Grand Lake Yacht Club's first Commodore. 1912 photo. (Courtesy Dorothy O'Ryan.)

gear for men consisted of a suit and tie with a pressed shirt and straw hat, while the ladies donned fashionable hats and long dresses. Sailing became a social occasion as much as a competitive one, part of the carefree summer lifestyle of boating and fishing, cocktail parties and cook-outs.

By the fall of 1911, Club members had raised enough money ($3,000) to construct a new clubhouse. Jake Pettingell graciously donated a beautiful plot of land near the North Inlet, Denver architect Arron Gove designed an elegant, functional structure, and in 1912 the new Grand Lake Yacht Club proudly opened its doors (to members only) on the north shore of the lake.

That same year, Club members convinced renowned tea magnate and avid yachtsman Sir Thomas Lipton to donate a sterling silver trophy for the Club's annual regatta, a rather impressive achievement for a tiny yacht club in the middle of Colorado that had existed for barely a decade.

The story of how the Grand Lakers actually managed to secure the Lipton Cup has several variations, but according to Dorothy O'Ryan's version, William Bryant was a member of the New York Yacht Club (even though he lived in Colorado), where he met Sir Thomas Lipton in either 1910 or 1911. Lipton, born in Glasgow to Irish parents in 1850,

Typical clothing for an early boat cruise on Grand Lake: dresses and hats for the ladies, suits and ties for the gentlemen. Grandview Hotel in the background. 1898 photo.
(Courtesy Denver Public Library, Western History Collection)

Well-dressed ladies and gentlemen fish for trout in this photograph entitled "After the Speckeled (sic) Beauties." Note the footbridge in the background. Engineers removed the large rock in the early 1940s as part of the Colorado-Big Thompson Project that turned the outlet into an inlet. 1892 photo.
(Courtesy Colorado Historical Society)

The brand-new Grand Lake Yacht Club, designed by Arron Gove and constructed on land donated by Jake Pettingell, 1912. (Courtesy Dorothy O'Ryan)

Another view of the new Yacht Club, looking toward the west, 1912. (Courtesy United States Geological Survey)

had earned his first million by age thirty with a chain of grocery stores. His investments in tea and rubber plantations, packing houses, and factories eventually earned him world-wide fame and a considerable fortune. He spent most of his later years traveling the globe, donating money to worthy charities and indulging his passion for yacht racing, which explains his presence at the New York Yacht Club. William Bryant shrewdly fueled that passion with dazzling tales of a yacht club high in the mountains of Colorado on the shores of a beautiful lake, where the sailing challenged even the most seasoned off-shore racers. Intrigued, Lipton agreed to visit when his schedule permitted.

Lipton kept his promise, at least partially. Due to his busy schedule, Lipton arrived in Denver in early December 1912, far too late to experience Grand Lake in all of its summer glory. Undeterred, Bryant and his fellow yacht clubbers joined with members of the distinguished Denver Club and the equally-prominent University Club to host a magnificent dinner in honor of Sir Lipton at the Denver Club on December 3, 1912. The lavish menu, printed in French, included lobster, caviar, and vintage French champagne, and the cream of Denver's social elite showed up in elaborate nautical uniforms. Lipton is reported to have said later that he'd never seen so many commodores in his life. Amid all of the pomp and pageantry and endless toasting, the Grand Lakers evidently plied Lipton with enough champagne (he was Irish, after all) to elicit a promise that he would donate a silver trophy cup to the Grand Lake Yacht Club.

Sir Thomas Lipton never made it to Grand Lake, but his cup arrived as promised, securely packed in an enormous wooden crate. William Bryant reportedly brought the crate to his Denver home and playfully informed his daughter Dorothy (Dorothy O'Ryan's mother) that the crate was actually a baby's coffin. The macabre charade ended when Bryant opened the crate to reveal an exquisite, elaborately inlaid sterling silver cup nestled in a bed of velvet. Ever since, Grand Lake's sailors have competed for the Lipton Cup during the Yacht Club's annual Regatta Week in August. The race for silver in the mountains had been replaced by a race for silver on the lake.

Aerial view of the annual Grand Lake Yacht Club Regatta. Photo circa late 1980s. (Courtesy James family, Grand Lake Lodge)

An E-scow screams across Grand Lake during the annual Regatta. 1989 photo. (Author photo)

*Looking due east down Grand Avenue near the turn of the century.
With a solid tourist infrastructure already in place, Grand Lake
survived while the mining camps along the North Fork turned into
ghost towns. Photo by Dalgleish, circa 1898.* (Courtesy Denver Public
Library, Western History Collection)

*A courageous hound braves the footbridge over the outlet while boaters
enjoy a pleasant cruise. Photo circa 1898.* (Courtesy Grand County
Historical Association Museum)

The Grand Lake Mercantile Company, 1908. As Grand Lake prospered in the early 1900s, larger buildings such as this became more common. Note the large tent to the left. (Courtesy Denver Public Library, Western History Collection)

An exquisite photograph of the outlet, taken by L.C. McClure circa 1915. McClure produced a number of stunning images of Grand Lake. (Denver Public Library, Western History Collection)

*Another McClure photograph, showing a dock and sailboat
on the south shore of the lake with the Rabbit Ears Range
in the distance (not to be confused with Rabbit Ears Pass
on the western edge of North Park). Photo circa 1912.*
(Courtesy Denver Public Library, Western History
Collection)

Sailors vie for a variety of prestigious cups during
Regatta Week, but the Lipton Cup is the Holy Grail of Grand
Lake sailing, the trophy that confers supreme honors and a
full year of bragging rights to the captain and crew that
manage to master the lake's notoriously temperamental
waters. Although comparatively diminutive in size, Grand
Lake can be exceedingly difficult to sail; the rugged
mountains and canyons surrounding it often create swirling,
unpredictable winds that challenge and deceive even the
most experienced mariners. Careless sailors are usually
rewarded with capsized boats and frigid immersion in the
lake's hypothermia-inducing water. Calm and placid one
moment, a churning maelstrom of foaming whitecaps the
next, Grand Lake has humbled several generations of sailors
who dared to underestimate its eccentricities.

By 1915, roughly thirty years after the mining bust left ghost towns scattered along the North Fork, Grand Lake had confidently stepped back from the brink of economic oblivion. The lake's reputation for excellent hunting, fishing, and boating had emerged intact; the foundations of a robust tourist industry were firmly in place; wealthy professionals and business people from Denver and the Midwest continued to build summer cabins on the shores of the lake; and the recent explosive growth in automobile ownership (spurred largely by the success of the Ford Model T) brought ever increasing numbers of tourists to the region.

Granted, tourism remained strictly a seasonal affair as tourists flocked to Grand Lake during the summer, then virtually disappeared with the first flakes of winter, leaving the little town to slip into hibernation until the cycle began again with the spring thaw. Nonetheless, Grand Lake had not only survived but actually prospered, thanks primarily to the astonishing beauty of the town's location and to the dedication and perseverance of its pioneering citizens.

CHAPTER NINE

PRESERVATION AND PROGRESS

In 1872, two years before William Henry Jackson took his first photographs of Grand Lake, President Ulysses S. Grant signed legislation designating over two million acres of northwestern Wyoming as Yellowstone National Park, thereby ensuring federal protection of the land "for the benefit and enjoyment of the people." It was the world's first instance of large-scale wilderness preservation in the public interest, and marked the beginning of the end for the heady frontier days of endless abundance and rapacious extraction, when pioneer miners, loggers, and settlers simply took what they needed from nature and left ravaged landscapes in their wake. As the nineteenth century drew to a close, a new conservation ethic, inspired in part by the writings of Henry David Thoreau and Scottish naturalist John Muir, the paintings of Albert Bierstadt and Thomas Moran, and the pioneering landscape photographs of W.H. Jackson, led to an increase in public support for protection of America's wilderness regions. One of the most vocal and eloquent proponents of this new ethic was Enos Mills, a tireless advocate for nature who led the campaign to establish Rocky Mountain National Park.

An abiding fascination with the great outdoors defined the life of Enos Mills. Born in Kansas in 1870, Mills first came to Colorado in 1884. Captivated by the alpine splendor of Estes Park region, he began spending his summers guiding and climbing in the region. After his first ascent at age fifteen, Mills eventually summitted Longs Peak over 250 times. A chance meeting with John Muir on a beach near San Francisco inspired Enos Mills to dedicate himself to the preservation of nature, and the mountains of northern Colorado became the focus of his quest.

Estes Park's spectacular scenery, coupled with its proximity to the population centers of the Front Range, virtually guaranteed its growth as a tourist destination. By the first decade of the twentieth century, the rapidly increasing numbers of vacationers and summer residents (and the hotels and other businesses that catered to them) motivated Mills and several other prominent citizens of Estes Park to lobby for protection of the very resource that attracted all of those tourists in the first place, the region's wilderness and wildlife. Mills threw himself into the effort with typical determination. He lectured widely, wrote endless letters, and helped establish the Colorado Mountain Club to spread his gospel of preservation. Despite opposition to his plans from various landowners and those concerned about government interference in local affairs, the efforts of Mills and his constituents finally paid off in January 1915, when President Woodrow Wilson signed a bill authorizing creation of Rocky Mountain National Park. It was not a total

Enos Mills and his dog Scotch. Mills led the campaign to establish Rocky Mountain National Park. President Woodrow Wilson signed legislation creating the park in January 1915. Photo circa 1914. (Courtesy RMNPHC)

victory for Mills, however; the bill created a park of 385.5 square miles, roughly a third of what he had envisioned. The park eventually grew to 415.2 square miles, or approximately 266,000 acres.

While Grand Lakers didn't play much of a role in the campaign to establish the park (historian Robert Black referred to Grand County's response as "lackadaisical"), they certainly stood to benefit from its creation. The impending completion of a new automobile road linking Estes Park and Grand Lake led to wide-eyed excitement over the expected increase in tourist visits, and since the boundaries for the new park carefully excluded private property around Grand Lake, the town would maintain control over its own destiny and yet also reap the rewards of having a national park as a neighbor. In essence, Rocky Mountain National Park guaranteed Grand Lake's economic future.

SQUEAKY BOB

Legislation authorizing Rocky Mountain National Park also guaranteed citizens the right to maintain ownership of any private property that ended up inside the new park's boundaries. Perhaps the most famous and surely the most colorful of these citizens was Robert L. "Squeaky Bob" Wheeler. Born in Michigan in 1865, Wheeler first came to Colorado in 1885 at the age of twenty to work on his brother Luke's ranch in North Park, where he learned the ways of the West and earned the nickname that stuck with him for the rest of his life. At age eighteen, Bob suffered a severe attack of bronchitis which left him with a distinct "squeak" in his voice. Barely noticeable at normal conversational levels, the squeak got progressively louder and more pronounced as Bob raised his voice, which he did often, usually in a stream of impossibly colorful profanity. Fellow cowboys began referring to him as Squeaky. Surprisingly, Bob actually liked the nickname. In his mind, it was far superior to his previous nickname of "Tenderfoot," and he even took to signing his checks "Squeaky Bob."

Robert L. "Squeaky Bob" Wheeler with his dog Jack. Wheeler operated the popular Camp Wheeler (also known as Squeaky Bob's Place, or the Hotel de Hardscrabble) at the base of Milner Pass, about fourteen miles north of Grand Lake. Famous for his cooking, tall tales, and impossibly colorful profanity, Squeaky Bob operated his resort until 1926, when poor health forced him to move to Denver. He passed away in 1945. Note Jack's sunglasses. Photo circa 1916. (Courtesy RMNPHC)

In 1892 Squeaky Bob signed a contract to break three hundred wild horses for two men who planned to ship them to New York City to pull street cars. Bob hired a couple of cowboys who helped him break most of the horses, but one afternoon a particularly vicious bronco kicked at Bob and pinned his right hand against a wagon, nearly severing two fingers. With no medical help nearby, Wheeler simply took out his knife and cut off the now useless fingers. The episode gave Squeaky Bob Wheeler a gold mine of material for future tall tales. Sometime later he homesteaded 160 acres near the North Fork of the Colorado River in an area that became known as Phantom Valley, about fourteen miles north of Grand Lake at the foot of Milner Pass.

In 1898 Wheeler enlisted in the cavalry to fight in the Spanish-American War. He served seven months with Colonel Torry's Rough Riders but never saw combat, spending most of his time tending horses near Jacksonville, Florida. Never overly fond of the truth, Squeaky Bob seldom bothered to correct the mistaken assumption that he had fought at San Juan Hill with Teddy Roosevelt's Rough Riders, although his cousin, General Joseph "Fighting Joe" Wheeler, did in fact ride with Roosevelt.

Bob returned to his homestead along the North Fork in 1900 and set about improving his cabin. He spent his days hunting and trapping, tending a few head of cattle, and prospecting in the nearby mountains. In 1908 guide Shep Husted of Estes Park convinced Bob to open a summer resort. Husted wanted a place to bring his increasingly popular horseback tours for a good meal and a warm bed, and Wheeler obliged by erecting four tents and dishing up what soon became world famous food. The printed signs that Bob hung in his tents typified the atmosphere of his establishment: "Blow your nose and clean your shoes. Use all the grub you need and leave things as you find them."

By the end of the first season the resort had grown to twenty tents. Business continued to accelerate in subsequent years, fueled largely by rumors of Bob's fabulous cooking and tall tales. He even put out a brochure describing the rustic amenities of "Camp Wheeler, Squeaky Bob's Place on the Colorado River, Hotel de Hardscrabble, where nature is still unspoiled." Word of the tent resort traveled fast, and before long Squeaky Bob's Place had an international reputation. Teddy Roosevelt stopped by on a hunting trip, as did English lords and legions of tourists traveling on horseback from Estes or bouncing in wagons along the bumpy road from Grand Lake. Squeaky Bob eventually married one of his housekeepers and ran his resort until 1926, when heart trouble forced him to sell and move to a lower elevation. "I'm in the winter of my life now," said Squeaky, "and like the sheep I had to come down from the high country." Squeaky Bob Wheeler died in Denver in 1945, his legend secure as one of Grand Lake's all-time characters. His property went through various owners and guises before evolving into the Phantom Valley Ranch, a popular dude ranch. The National Park Service eventually acquired the property and tore everything down in an attempt to restore the site to its natural state.

HIGH ROADS

The creation of Rocky Mountain National Park promised a secure future for tourism in Grand Lake, and Fall River Road delivered the tourists necessary to fulfill that promise. Serious discussions for a road linking Grand Lake with Estes Park had developed as early as 1895, but work on the project did not commence until 1913, nearly two years before the creation of the national park. In September of that year, selected convicts from the Colorado State Penitentiary moved into cabins along Fall River near Estes and began the seven-year road project that would span the Continental Divide and allow, for the first time, automobile traffic to travel between Estes Park and Grand Lake during the summer months. The route chosen for the road essentially followed the old Arapaho Dog's Trail: from Horseshoe Park up Fall River to Fall River Pass (near the present-day Alpine Visitor Center), then over the Continental Divide at Poudre Lake (now called Milner Pass, named for surveyor T.J. Milner), down a series of steep switchbacks to the floor of the Kawuneeche (North Fork) Valley, and on to Grand Lake.

On the west side, contractor Dick McQueary and Grand County civil engineer/surveyor Franklin Huntington had plotted a feasible route from Milner Pass to the North Fork in one day in 1912. In 1915, as work slowed dramatically on the Estes side of the project due to controversies over the use of convict labor, the Grand County Commissioners hired McQueary to upgrade the badly rutted road between Grand Lake and Squeaky Bob's Place. Two years later McQueary received another contract to extend the road five and a half

*Construction crew working on the west side of Fall
River Road, just above present-day Fairview Curve.
Kawuneeche Valley and the Never Summer Mountains
in the distance. Photo circa 1918.* (Courtesy
RMNPHC)

miles up steep terrain to Milner Pass. This section of the
road required nine switchbacks and earned the nickname
"Giant's Ladder." McQueary's crews finished preliminary
grading of the precipitous west side of the road by June 1918
despite labor shortages caused by World War I, and the
completed road finally opened in September 1920.

Controversy surrounded the construction of Fall River
Road. In addition to the furor over convict labor, the National
Park Service awarded Roe Emery's Rocky Mountain Parks
Transportation Company exclusive rights to haul sightseeing
passengers through the park in 1919. This virtual monopoly
came in response to numerous complaints about
unscrupulous, independent tour operators cheating their
customers with inflated prices and shoddy transportation
services. Seeking "the greatest good for the greatest number
of visitors," the Park Service simply eliminated all
competition for public transportation in the park.

Local entrepreneurs in Estes Park and Grand Lake responded with outrage. Enos Mills was especially vocal in his opposition: "Our national park policy governs without the consent of the governed." Mills arranged for unauthorized drivers to enter the park in order to test the new policy, which of course led to arrests, more acrimony, and eventually lawsuits. Another factor complicated the issue: Fall River Road as well as other roads in the Park had been built with state and local money (Grand and Larimer counties), yet the federal government took over control of the road upon its completion. Not until 1929 did Colorado officially relinquish its rights to park roads.

Despite the turmoil, Fall River Road proved to be an immense success. Visits to the park jumped dramatically, from 120,000 visitors in 1917 to 240,966 in 1920, inspiring local NPS officials to boast that Rocky Mountain drew more people "than the combined tourist patronage of Yellowstone, Yosemite, Glacier, and Crater Lake Parks." The park's proximity to Denver and easy rail accessibility from the East and Midwest ensured its popularity, and also encouraged dozens of new tourist-oriented businesses to open on both sides of the Divide. John G. Holzworth and his family followed Squeaky Bob's lead and opened the Holzworth Trout Lodge (later known as the Never Summer Ranch) in the Kawuneeche Valley in 1920. Other rustic resorts including the Green Mountain Ranch and the Harbison Dude Ranch also prospered. The spectacular Grand Lake Lodge, with its incomparable view of Grand Lake, opened two months prior to the road in order to be ready for the expected caravans of tourists.

Roe Emery, the "Father of Colorado Tourism," had envisioned the Grand Lake Lodge as an integral component of his ambitious "Circle Tour." Tourists from all over the country and the world would board buses at train depots in Denver, Greeley, and Lyons, then travel to Estes Park for a night in Emery's Estes Park Chalet. The following day, guests again boarded buses for the breathtaking ride up

Fall River Road over the roof of the continent, reaching an elevation of 11,796 feet. The road, though scenic, was both rugged and dangerous, characterized by numerous switchbacks with "exceedingly sharp curves," frighteningly steep grades, and narrow roadbeds that prohibited safe two-way travel in some sections. Busloads of guests invariably heaved a collective sigh of relief when they pulled into Grand Lake Lodge on the west side of the park, where grand views, good food, and comfortable (if Spartan) accommodations awaited. After a night's rest and breakfast in the Lodge, the tour buses headed south, crested Berthoud Pass, and arrived in Idaho Springs to spend one more night in another Emery property, the Hot Springs Hotel. The next morning the buses returned to the Mile High City of Denver, thus completing the famous Circle Tour. Variations on this tour continue to be popular among contemporary travelers.

Heavy traffic and vicious winter weather combined to make maintenance on the Fall River Road an absolute nightmare. Washouts were common, and traffic jams caused by the narrow road and steep grades frazzled more than a few nerves and automobile transmissions. Finally, after the State of Colorado ceded its rights to roads in the park in February 1929, the National Park Service announced plans for an even more ambitious and scenic road to replace the Fall River route.

Congress appropriated $450,000 for the new road in April 1929. By October W.A. Colt had secured the contract for construction on the east side. Work began immediately with power shovels and tractors supplementing Colt's crew of 185 men. Colt instructed his men to take extra care not to damage the fragile tundra environment of the new route, which roughly followed the old Ute Indian Child's Trail and included an eleven-mile stretch above timberline that offered staggering vistas in every direction. As with the Fall River Project, a separate contractor (L.T. Lawler) began work on the west side. Despite the lofty elevations and fierce weather, construction proceeded rapidly, and in 1932 Trail Ridge

Road, elevation 12,183 feet at its highest point, opened for business. Eventually the NPS paved the entire road, which earned Trail Ridge the distinction of being the highest continuous paved road in the United States.

Now more accessible than ever, Grand Lake seemed primed for a tremendous growth in tourism, but the economic realities of the Great Depression and fear generated by the dark clouds of war gathering over Europe in the middle and late 1930s kept business down. Once again, however, the federal government stepped in, this time with detailed plans for an impressive transmountain water diversion project that not only helped Grand Lake weather the economic uncertainties of the Depression and subsequent World War, but also enhanced its already impressive reputation for recreational opportunities.

THE COLORADO-BIG THOMPSON PROJECT

The Continental Divide effectively separates Colorado into two distinct climatological regions. The mountainous West Slope, home to roughly twenty percent of the state's population, receives nearly seventy percent of the state's moisture. The East Slope, on the other hand, receives barely thirty percent of the state's moisture, yet it contains nearly eighty percent of the state's population, the vast majority concentrated in the urbanized Front Range corridor from Fort Collins in the north to Trinidad in the south. Consequently, Colorado's history abounds with ambitious plans to bring West Slope water to the population centers and industries of the Front Range, as well as to the fertile soils and thirsty farms and ranches of the eastern plains. Not surprisingly, these same plans have also created enormous hostility between rival factions vying for control of the state's limited water supplies. It is a classic struggle in the arid American West: those who have water want to protect their most precious resource from those who do not.

Water engineers first eyed Grand Lake as a potential water supply for the Front Range as early as 1889. Plans

Aerial view of Trail Ridge Road looking south-southwest. The highest continuous paved road in the United States, Trail Ridge Road replaced the old Fall River Road in 1932. Medicine Bow Curve at bottom of photo, Alpine Visitor Center and Trail Ridge Store at middle left. Undated photo. (Courtesy RMNPHC)

Three Coleman buses and a La Salle Phaeton (convertible) loaded with passengers for the spectacular ride over Trail Ridge. 1935 photo. (Courtesy James family, Grand Lake Lodge)

called for a series of diversion ditches similar to the Grand Ditch to transport water from Grand Lake over the Divide to South Boulder Creek. Rugged terrain and high cost estimates doomed the project, but another plan soon appeared for a twelve-mile tunnel that would tap Grand Lake and divert the water to the Big Thompson or St. Vrain rivers. In very general terms, this plan first outlined the basics for what eventually became the Colorado-Big Thompson Project (C-BT). Again, high costs and engineering difficulties shelved the proposal. In 1904, the newly formed Reclamation Service began investigating a plan to enlarge Grand Lake by damming the outlet and diverting the North Fork into the lake, thereby raising water levels as much as twenty-five feet. Like the others, this project was eventually abandoned, but Grand Lake would undoubtedly be a very different place if the plan had ever reached fruition.

Continued growth in Colorado kept the quest for West Slope water alive. By the 1930s new technologies and increased demand combined to resurrect the idea for a water-diversion tunnel through the Continental Divide. Complicated political and legal maneuvering ensued, but by 1937 the newly formed Northern Colorado Water Conservancy District (NCWCD) and the federal Bureau of Reclamation (BOR) had hammered out the details of the massive project. In essence, the C-BT project called for a West Slope collection system of four reservoirs, four dams, two pumping plants, and miles of associated canals and waterways that would capture water from the high mountains of the upper Colorado River region, store it, regulate it, and then transport it to Grand Lake for diversion through a tunnel to the Front Range.

In December 1938 construction began on the first phase of the project, the Green Mountain Dam and Reservoir south of Kremmling. As part of the legislation authorizing the C-BT, the BOR had agreed to build Green Mountain Reservoir in order to store enough water to offset or replace water diverted to the East Slope, sort of an insurance plan for wary West Slopers who feared they would lose all of their water to the Front Range. Despite labor shortages and financial hardships associated with the outbreak of World War II, construction on all phases of the C-BT proceeded during the late 1930s and early 1940s.

Construction on the crucial tunnel between Grand Lake and Estes Park began on the east side of the project with a ceremonial dynamite blast on June 23, 1940. Work proceeded quickly through stable granite on the east side, but unstable gneiss and schist hampered excavation efforts on the west side. When World War II threatened to delay the entire project, supporters convinced Congress that the C-BT would generate power for the war effort and food for the populace. Work continued, and on June 10, 1944, four days after allied forces landed in Normandy, the final bore-through connected the two ends of the 13.1-mile tunnel. A quick survey revealed that the two ends were off by one-sixteenth of an inch on the center line and three-fourths of an inch on the grade, an impressive achievement for a project 3,800 feet under the crest of the Continental Divide. Six months later, President Franklin Roosevelt signed legislation officially naming the tunnel after Senator Alva B. Adams, a Democrat from Pueblo who was instrumental in securing federal funding for the project. Water first flowed through the concrete-lined, 9.75 foot diameter tunnel on June 23, 1947. Just as Fall River Road had linked Grand Lake and Estes Park over the Continental Divide, the Adams Tunnel now linked them beneath it.

Upon final completion of the project in 1959, the Western Slope Collection System of the C-BT was capable of diverting up to 310,000 acre-feet of water from the West Slope to the East. Lake Granby, an enormous reservoir created when the Granby Dam interrupted the flow of the Colorado River about seven miles northeast of the town of Granby, is the principal storage facility of the project, supplemented by water from Willow Creek Reservoir. At the north end of Lake Granby a huge pumping plant lifts water 125 feet into the

Colorado-Big Thompson Western Slope Collection System. (Courtesy Northern Colorado Water Conservancy District)

Granby Pump Canal, which transports the water to Shadow Mountain Reservoir, a shallow, man-made lake that acts as a sort of shock absorber to prevent dramatic water level fluctuations in Grand Lake. From Shadow Mountain, water flows by gravity through a connecting channel to Grand Lake, where an intake structure at the east end of the lake diverts water into the Alva B. Adams Tunnel for the nearly three-hour journey to Estes Park. From Estes, water once destined for the Pacific Ocean is transported to the cities, industries, farms, and ranches of northeastern Colorado.

Ironically, because the Northern Colorado Water Conservancy District refused to pay more than the $25 million it had contracted for the project, the Bureau of Reclamation decided against sending water down the project's namesake, the Big Thompson Canyon. Instead, a series of pipes and canals diverted the water through two power stations to help cover the cost of the project, which eventually reached $160 million.

Aside from being the largest of Colorado's thirty-seven transmountain water diversion projects, the Colorado-Big Thompson Project had a profound impact upon Grand Lake. Economically, construction payrolls generated by the project helped keep local businesses solvent during the lean years of the 1930s and 1940s. In addition, the creation of Lake Granby and Shadow Mountain Reservoir greatly enhanced the region's fishing, boating, and recreational opportunities, which in turn led to an increase in the construction of new summer cabins, marinas, campgrounds, hotels, and a myriad of other businesses and facilities, all designed to cater to the legions of tourists expected to visit what became known as the Great Lakes of Colorado. By 1960, with the massive lakes created by the C-BT to its south and Rocky Mountain National Park to its north and east, Grand Lake found itself smack in the middle of one of the nation's prime tourist destinations.

The C-BT increased knowledge of Grand Lake's prehistoric past through legislation that required detailed archaeological excavations in areas that would be inundated by the project's reservoirs. Scientists discovered a number of Paleolithic and historic Indian sites in the regions now covered by Lake Granby and Willow Creek and Shadow Mountain reservoirs. Information and artifacts gleaned from these scattered sites helped clarify the region's pre-European Contact history. Unfortunately, the water that eventually covered them also submerged a number of historic ranches and homesteads located along the Colorado River. Like the river itself, these places simply disappeared with the rising waters of the Colorado-Big Thompson Project.

The completion of the C-BT also closed a significant chapter in the history of Grand Lake. For centuries, Grand Lake (in conjunction with the North Fork) had been considered the traditional headwaters of the mighty Colorado, the dynamic river that carved the incomparable Grand Canyon and played such a crucial role in the exploration and eventual settlement of the American West. The outlet of Grand Lake in particular achieved an almost mythical status as the symbolic beginning of the river. Indians had fished in it, Grand Lake's first permanent resident had settled next to it, famous travelers such as William Byers, John Wesley Powell, and William Henry Jackson had camped nearby, and the outlet figured prominently in early maps and descriptions of the lake. When modern technology and some rather remarkable

A cloud partially obscures Grand Lake in this aerial view looking southwest. The outlet and the Colorado River valley are clearly visible in the middle and upper right of the photograph. Shadow Mountain Lake, part of the Colorado-Big Thompson Project, inundated this valley in the late 1940s. Shadow Mountain at upper left, Summerland Park at middle bottom. 1921 photo. (Courtesy RMNPHC)

engineering reversed the flow of the Colorado River and transformed the outlet into an inlet, Grand Lake lost an important element of its history forever. In addition, the C-BT flooded the confluence

The Corner Cupboard, circa 1931. The King of Iraq dined here in 1952 while on a tour of the Colorado-Big Thompson Project. (Courtesy Aron Rhone)

of the North Fork and the Grand Lake outlet, another historic sacrifice for the sake of dependable water supplies for distant cities and farms.

A final historic footnote to the C-BT saga concerns a royal visit to Grand Lake. In August 1952, His Majesty King Faisal II of Iraq arrived with his staff for an official tour of the project. Faisal had assumed the Iraqi throne at age three after his father, King Ghazi I, died in a car crash in 1939. At the time of his visit, Faisal was not yet eighteen and therefore had not officially taken over the country, but his ascension ceremony had been scheduled for the following May. John Henry Rhone, a lifelong resident of Grand Lake, remembers the king and his staff dining at his father Henry's Corner Cupboard restaurant. Rhone also remembers a boat cruise that almost touched off an international incident.

At one point during the king's visit, the fifteen-year-old Rhone and the seventeen-year-old king slipped away from the rest of the entourage and "borrowed" a small boat for a cruise around the lake. The spectacular mountain scenery absolutely dazzled the young king, who at one point wished aloud that he could remain in Grand Lake while Rhone returned to the deserts of the Middle East in his place. The

King Faisal II of Iraq (seated fourth from left) and his entourage dine with U.S. State Department officials at the Corner Cupboard, August 1952. The king and young John Henry Rhone later took a boat ride that almost touched off an international incident. (Courtesy Aron Rhone)

king also offered to trade "a whole stable of Arabians" for John Henry's pinto horse, an offer that Rhone politely refused. The Grand Lake resident and the boy-king continued their cruise, unaware that Iraqi and U.S. State Department officials were frantic about the unprecedented breach of security the two boys had caused with their little adventure. In desperation, U.S. and Iraqi security agents launched an exhaustive search of the lake.

Finally, Rhone and the king returned on their own (much to the chagrin of the security forces) and were welcomed with stern reprimands and admonitions from both governments. The much feared international incident never materialized, and King Faisal II and his staff eventually returned to Iraq. Six years later, in July 1958, a military coup led by General Karim Kassem toppled the Iraqi monarchy and killed King Faisal. Later, jubilant Iraqis dragged the king's lifeless body through the streets of Baghdad, and John Henry Rhone thanked his lucky stars that he had decided to remain in his beloved Grand Lake.

A TOWN FOR ALL SEASONS

Generations of families like the Rhones have witnessed the monumental changes brought by continued growth and development in Grand Lake. Longtime residents still get misty-eyed remembering Zick's Motel and Grocery, the Pine Cone Inn, the venerable old Corner Cupboard, or dancing at the Little Bear. Dozens of other businesses have come and gone over the years, testimony to the fact that merely locating in Grand Lake is not enough to guarantee success. Other establishments—the Lariat Saloon, the Chuckhole Cafe, Humphrey's Store—have managed to prosper through a combination of hard work, innovation, and repeat business from loyal customers, and each has added its own contributions to the stability of the local economy and the local community.

Until very recently, many of Grand Lake's successful businesses relied almost entirely on the brief summer tourist season for the majority of their revenue. The pattern had become fairly well established. Spring never attracted many tourists ("mud season," the locals call it) but business absolutely boomed during the summer, with the annual Buffalo Barbecue Days, the popular Fourth of July fireworks display, the Yacht Club Regatta, and other special events helping to maximize the profit margin for local businesses. Then, inevitably, tourists began dwindling as the aspens

A wooden Indian stands watch over the boardwalk in front of the Lariat Saloon and the Grand Lake Pharmacy. Grand Lake's popularity as a tourist destination continues to grow. 1997 photo. (Author photo)

A snowmobiler cruises down Grand Avenue. Grand Lake bills itself as the "Snowmobile Capital of Colorado," a distinction that has generated both considerable revenue and controversy for the town. 1997 photo. (Author photo)

started turning in a remarkable riot of autumn colors. By the time winter arrived, many establishments simply closed for the season, their inventories depleted, their workers gone for the ski towns of Winter Park, Steamboat, or Vail. Local residents settled in for a long winter of deep snow and ice on their windshields.

That pattern has changed considerably over the last decade or so. Spring is still muddy and wet, summer still booms with tourists, and autumn is still the region's best kept secret, but winter has become exceedingly profitable in Grand Lake, thanks to the surging popularity of snowmobiling. A vigorous chamber of commerce campaign and a vast network of trails has transformed Grand Lake into the "Snowmobile Capital of Colorado," much to the delight of local business owners. Hotels and restaurants that used to struggle to survive during the winter are now thronged with snowmobile enthusiasts, and on busy weekends the town boasts more snowmobiles than automobiles.

A snowmobile "drag race" across the frozen surface of Grand Lake. The town has experienced a tremendous increase in snowmobiling over the last decade. 1997 photo. (Author photo)

Not everyone, it seems, is pleased with the transformation. Accidents involving inexperienced riders on machines that can reach upwards of one hundred miles per hour have nearly tripled over the last few years, including a number of fatal crashes and one incident in which four sleds cracked through the ice covering one of the lakes and sank to the bottom. Local residents are angry about the high-powered snowmobiles tearing through their once quiet neighborhoods at all hours of the day and night. Perhaps more ominously, the flourishing popularity of snowmobiling has produced a distinct blue haze over the lake, a gauzy curtain of smog that obscures the very scenery that attracts people to Grand Lake in the first place. In response to the controversy, the city council formed a snowmobile advisory task force to examine the situation and suggest possible compromises. Most everyone seems confident that solutions for the current dilemma can be found without resorting to shootouts on the shore.

From nomadic Paleo-Indians to modern tourists in motor homes, Grand Lake has weathered over ten thousand years of human history, and yet time has been kind to the little town with the turbulent past. The area's indigenous populations may be long gone, but William Byers' "great mirror" still reflects the lofty peaks covered in thick carpets of verdant timber, spectral mists still rise from the lake on sultry summer mornings, and hundreds of square miles of undeveloped wilderness teeming with wildlife continue to enchant visitors from all over the world. In this respect Grand Lake has changed little since its humble beginnings as Judge Joseph Wescott's personal playground.

Unlike bustling, traffic-clogged Estes Park or exclusive Colorado ski towns such as Aspen and Vail, Grand Lake has also managed to stay well below the radar of corporate America and the unpredictable, often negative impacts of large-scale commercial development. Such a position undoubtedly makes it difficult for small businesses to survive and prosper, yet most Grand Lake residents stubbornly resist corporate investment and the relentless economic forces that have irreparably transformed so many other Colorado mountain towns. The absence of valet parking, corporate theme restaurants, and glamorous shopping malls may disappoint and inconvenience some visitors, but locals clearly recognize that Grand Lake's lack of high-priced amenities helps preserve their little slice of paradise.

Regardless of what the future holds for Grand Lake, the region's astonishing natural beauty will continue to endure, thanks in large part to the efforts of visionary citizens and lawmakers who had the tremendous wisdom and foresight to establish Rocky Mountain National Park and the Arapaho National Forest. Meanwhile, despite the fires and fueds, the shootouts and snowslides, the booms and the busts, and even a dubious flirtation with legalized gambling, Colorado's oldest tourist destination has somehow managed to retain its unspoiled charm. Change may be inevitable, but the lake and the trees and the mountains have remained constant, providing a tangible connection between contemporary Grand Lake and its rich and storied past. It is, undeniably, a past that deserves to be remembered, set in a landscape that deserves to be protected.

CHAPTER TEN

THE GRAND LAKE LODGE

For a town that is still decades away from celebrating its one hundred and fiftieth birthday, Grand Lake has lost an astonishing number of historic hotels. Wilson Waldron's Grand Lake House is long gone. So too are the Fairview House, the Grand Central Hotel, the Grandview, the Rustic Hotel, the Bellevue Hotel, and the Pine Cone Inn. The Kauffman House still stands on the shores of Grand Lake, although it hasn't had many overnight guests lately. Even Squeaky Bob Wheeler's Hotel de Hardscrabble has disappeared, along with the boom towns and the dude ranches that shared the Kawuneeche Valley. All of these structures played some role in the history of Grand Lake, and most of them are gone forever.

One hotel property that managed to avoid the depressing fate suffered by so many of Grand Lake's historic structures is the Grand Lake Lodge. Since 1920, the Lodge has perched like a sentinel on the hillside north of town, an elegant building from a long vanished era, blessed with an incomparable, absolutely commanding view of the town below and the lake and mountains beyond. The thickly timbered, seventy-acre Lodge property, which is bordered on the north, west, and east by Rocky Mountain National Park, includes over one hundred buildings, the vast majority of which are cabins designed for overnight accommodation. For over seventy-five years, the Lodge has welcomed guests from all over the world who come to experience its enchanting blend of wilderness and history. The fact that the facility continues to operate successfully as a seasonal business is testimony to its owners' continuing commitment to preserve and protect one of the few remaining hotels from Grand Lake's remarkable past.

The history of the Grand Lake Lodge actually dates to 1917, when RMNP Chief Ranger (later Superintendent)

Very early photograph of the Grand Lake Lodge, circa 1922. This popular facility opened with a Grand Ball on July 3, 1920. It is now a National Historic Landmark. Note the American flag hanging from the peeled log structure (known as a pergola) over the stairs. (Courtesy RMNPHC)

L.Claude Way and Ranger Howard G. Beehler (the sole ranger on the park's west side, known to Grand Lake residents as "The Timber Beast") located a level site for a large "camp" at the edge of the park overlooking Grand Lake. The "camp" never materialized, but within three years a more elegant structure occupied the scenic site, thanks largely to the efforts of Roe Emery, who had experienced considerable success operating a bus line in Glacier National Park. His business acumen so impressed the representatives of several western railroads serving Denver, Greeley, Fort Collins, and Longmont that they approached him with proposals for similar services to carry rail passengers to Estes Park.

Emery agreed to coordinate bus service to Estes for the railroads and ended up purchasing three of the existing bus lines. He then replaced outdated buses and equipment and

Tourists admire the view from "Colorado's Favorite Front Porch." For over seventy-five years, the Grand Lake Lodge has welcomed visitors from all over he world. Photo circa 1922. (Courtesy RMNPHC)

launched his own Rocky Mountain Parks Transportation Company. Business initially proved marginal at best. In four years his bus lines lost $65,000. Undaunted, Emery stuck with it and finally hit pay dirt in 1919, when the National Park Service granted him a virtual monopoly for bus service through RMNP. With his guaranteed bus contract in hand, Emery persuaded a group of eastern capitalists to help finance construction of hotel accommodations for his passengers.

With work on the Fall River Road proceeding as planned, Emery wooed potential investors with his vision of an easy, affordable, and breathtaking Circle Tour of the Colorado Rockies. The package would include bus transportation from rail depots along the Front Range to Estes Park, Grand Lake, Idaho Springs, and back to Denver, with appropriate meals and accommodations at Emery's hotels along the way. The Estes Park Chalet and the Hot

Early visitors at the Grand Lake Lodge, July 1922. Maintenance crews evidently removed the peeled log pergola in the late 1920s or early 1930s. In a bit of historical irony, the daughter of the gentleman in the photo married a man named John Brownlee in 1940, brother of current Lodge owner Sue Brownlee James. (Courtesy James family, Grand Lake Lodge)

Springs Hotel in Idaho Springs partly satisfied the needs of his package tours, but Emery had trouble securing financing for the third jewel in his tourism Triple Crown, the Grand Lake Lodge. Finally, with help from A.D. Lewis of Hot Sulphur Springs and permission from the NPS to build on park property, work commenced on the last piece of Roe Emery's Circle Tour puzzle.

Facts pertaining to the actual construction of the Grand Lake Lodge are difficult to come by, but Frank Huntington (the Grand County surveyor who had earlier assisted Dick McQueary with Fall River Road) most likely surveyed the original "camp" site discovered by Way and Beehler, while at least one unverified source gives credit for designing the Lodge to a man named Al House. At any rate, in April 1919 horse-drawn freight wagons began hauling massive timber beams to the site from an old sawmill in Bowen Gulch.

Early photograph of the Grand Lake Lodge lobby area, showing the beautiful peeled log support posts and crossbeams. Note the circular fireplace (without a screen), the Front Desk beyond it, the hand-crafted furniture and Indian rugs, and the large bearskin on the wall to the right. Photo circa 1922. (Courtesy James family, Grand Lake Lodge)

Same view as previous photo, taken some years later. The circular fireplace has a screen around it, and a small gift shop now occupies the area to the right. The single center support posts visible in the older photo also appear to be have been replaced with new posts spaced farther apart. Photo circa 1926? (Courtesy James family, Grand Lake Lodge)

Additional timber (mostly lodgepole pine) was cut and rough-milled at a small sawmill located to the immediate north of the current Lodge property boundary (parts of this mill still exist). By June 1920 carpenters and craftsmen had nearly finished assembling the impressive main structure. Approximately one hundred and sixty feet long by sixty feet wide, constructed entirely from native materials, the main Lodge building boasted a high, open ceiling with beautiful hand-peeled support posts and crossbeams, hand-crafted hickory furniture, and a covered porch running the entire length of the building's south side. The Front Desk for the hotel stood at the west end of building, adjacent to a unique and functional circular fireplace, while a dining room and more traditional stone fireplace occupied the eastern half. Everywhere, it seemed, wondrous taxidermy highlighted the structure's natural wood and rustic yet elegant design.

North of the Lodge, crews constructed a small hydroelectric plant on the banks of Tonahutu Creek, then laid over a mile of power line and pipe to supply the entire property with electricity and water. Although the power plant has long since been abandoned, the original structure still stands and is currently being considered for renovation and designation as an historic site by the National Park Service. Tonahutu Creek continues to be the sole source of fresh water for the Grand Lake Lodge.

On July 3, 1920, just two months prior to the completion of the Fall River Road, the Grand Lake Lodge officially opened with a Grand Ball. The property proved to be an immediate hit with locals and tourists alike, due largely to its astonishing views and the undeniable ambiance of the main Lodge. Since this structure contained no overnight accommodations, construction continued on the small guest cabins nestled in the woods to the north and east of the main building. Within a few years the property contained over one hundred buildings, including a barn, a sawmill, numerous storage sheds, two large employee dormitories, and over seventy guest cabins, including the spacious Ford Cabin, where Henry Ford stayed in 1927.

Still, business did not quite meet expectations, and Roe Emery's financial backers threatened to close down the hotels that were so vital to the success of his bus business. Once again, Emery demonstrated his unwavering commitment to Colorado tourism by taking over the Estes Park Chalet, the Hot Springs Hotel, and the Grand Lake Lodge in 1927. Under his guidance the hotels and the bus line experienced tremendous success, so much so that Emery soon purchased a plot of land on Craig Point near the old Fairview House, where he planned to build another hotel. This particular hotel never materialized, but Emery's keen business sense ensured continued prosperity for his bus line and hotel properties for the next three decades.

Emery operated the Grand Lake Lodge as an integral part of his Circle Tour through the Depression years and World War II. In 1952 the seventy-eight year old "Father of Colorado Tourism" made the decision to retire. He sold his Rocky Mountain Parks Transportation Company to T.J. Manning of Denver. Manning, unable to secure adequate financing to complete the deal, offered the company to a

North side of Grand Lake Lodge lobby looking east. Gift shop to the left. Note the taxidermy. Photo circa 1926.
(Courtesy James family, Grand Lake Lodge)

Grand Lake Lodge circa 1950, with two "FLXBLE Glasstop" sightseeing buses parked in front. Buick automobile engines powered these buses that carried tourists on Roe Emery's famous Circle Tour. (Courtesy RMNPHC)

pair of hard-working brothers from Nebraska, Isaac B. and Ted L. James.

The opportunity offered by Manning proved to be an auspicious one for the James brothers. Each had extensive experience in the bus transportation business, and each sought new challenges in their respective careers. Realizing that Manning's financial distress resulted in an excellent bargaining position for them, the James brothers agreed to purchase the company and assumed control on January 1, 1953, forming a corporation under the name Colorado Transportation Company. As part of their deal with Manning, the James brothers did not purchase all of the Emery properties immediately. Instead, they had two leases with options to buy. After a successful first season in 1953, the James brothers exercised their option on one of the leases that included the Grand Lake Lodge and Trail Ridge Store at the top of Fall River Pass. Because the Lodge and Store

*Photograph taken in 1961 near present-day "Nuptial Knoll"
at Grand Lake Lodge, showing Lodge owners T.L. James
(left) and I.B. James (second from right) discussing plans to
exclude the Lodge from RMNP boundaries with (among
others) NPS director Conrad Wirth (second from left). Both
Congress and President John F. Kennedy approved the plan,
and in January 1963 the Grand Lake Lodge officially became
private property.* (Courtesy James family, Grand Lake
Lodge)

were both inside the park boundaries, the brothers
negotiated a twenty-year concessionaire contract with the
NPS for the period from 1955 to 1975. Ted L. James then
brought in his son Ted Jr. and his new bride Sue Brownlee
to operate Trail Ridge Store, while he looked after operations
at the Lodge and various other properties.

In 1961 the James brothers began negotiating with the
NPS to exclude the Grand Lake Lodge from park boundaries.
As part of the ambitious "Mission 66" program, the NPS
had launched a massive campaign to upgrade facilities and
remove private property (including all overnight
accommodations) from national parks across the country.
In some instances, Mission 66 planners implemented a
"scorched-earth" policy by simply buying properties inside
park boundaries and razing them. The policy unfortunately

led to the destruction of many historic structures in Rocky Mountain National Park, including, among others, the Fall River Lodge, Bear Lake Lodge, the Sprague Hotel, and the Glacier Basin Lodge. To save the Grand Lake Lodge from a similar fate, the James brothers acquired a number of private properties inside park boundaries and offered to exchange them for the land surrounding the Lodge.

Reluctant at first, the NPS eventually agreed to the land swap, although it took an act of Congress and the signature of President John F. Kennedy to authorize the boundary adjustment. Finally, in January 1963, the park officially moved its boundaries and the Grand Lake Lodge became the property of I.B. and T.L. James. Had they not been successful, it is possible that the NPS would have torn down the Grand Lake Lodge to restore the site to its natural state.

By June 1963 the James brothers agreed to divide their company, with I.B. assuming control of the bus operations and T.L. taking over the Lodge and other properties. Ted Jr. immediately joined his father and began managing the Lodge and Trail Ridge Store, staffing each with eager college students who kept things lively with their antics both on and off-duty. A new swimming pool in front of the Lodge became a welcome addition to the property and proved exceedingly popular with guests and employees alike, while good food and fabulous views continued to attract visitors from all over the world.

For the next several years the Lodge maintained its long-established pattern of catering to tourists during the brief summer season, then closing shortly after Labor Day. After the last tourists departed, a small crew shuttered the buildings and turned the power and water systems off. The property remained dormant through the long winter until the spring thaw began the cycle again. The business did marginally well, neither losing money nor making much, but more importantly, the Grand Lake Lodge had been saved from the Mission 66 demolition derby.

FIRE ON THE MOUNTAIN

On Thursday afternoon, July 19, 1973, in the very midst of the busy summer season, a cook began preparing for the nightly employee meal in the large kitchen located at the rear of the Grand Lake Lodge. Casually he fired up the brand new gas grill, covered it with steaks, and turned his attention elsewhere, unaware that he had set in motion a nearly catastrophic chain of events. It seems this new grill had all the latest gadgetry, including an innovative cleaning feature. With the push of a button, flames from the burners could be directed up through the grill to burn off any excess grease or fat. Unfamiliar with this feature, the cook had inadvertently pressed the cleaning button in order to cook his steaks, and within moments the grill had turned into a raging inferno.

With no fire suppression system in place, the flames quickly spread to the grill hood, then across the ceiling toward a clerestory (sort of a skylight) in the roof. The

Dramatic photograph of the Grand Lake Lodge dining room engulfed in flames, July 19, 1973. The fire closed the Lodge for seven years. (Courtesy James family, Grand Lake Lodge)

clerestory essentially became a huge chimney, fueling the flames and spreading them toward the dining room. Bob Scott, a dear friend of the James family and a longtime Lodge employee, happened to be on duty at the time and remembered the fire crackling and roaring, sounding like nothing so much as "French fries being dropped into hot grease." Before long the entire building began shaking from the combustion. Scott quickly instructed his wait staff to close the dining room windows, and then he and the rest of his restaurant crew began heaving the valuable, hand-crafted chairs onto the lawn below. Much of this furniture is still used in the Lodge dining room.

Within minutes the first elements of the local fire department arrived. Bob Scott and a handful of other employees continued to salvage rugs, taxidermy, and furniture as the dining room slowly filled with smoke. When it became apparent that the fire would not be extinguished quickly, the few employees still inside began evacuating. Scott remembered the entire building swaying like a ship on the high seas as the intricate lattice of support beams began flexing in the gathering heat. Employees and assorted guests assembled on the far end of the swimming pool and watched as a small battalion of firefighters began swarming over the back of the building, attempting to tackle the blaze at the source. A large engine parked on the front lawn quickly drained its water tank, with no apparent effect on the blaze.

Meanwhile, the temperature inside the Lodge continued to climb dramatically until it reached what firefighters refer to as the "flashover" point, when superheated air suddenly ignites all combustible material. An enormous explosion rocked the entire structure, blowing out the windows of the dining room and sending glowing fingers of orange flame out the front of the building and onto the roof. Bob Scott remembered glass from the blown-out windows flying over his head as he stood on the south edge of the swimming pool. Pieces of this glass can still be found on the hillside below the Lodge.

Smoke pours from the southwest end of the Grand Lake Lodge. Although the building sustained heavy damage, its structural integrity remained intact. (Courtesy James family, Grand Lake Lodge)

Employees and guests watched in stunned horror as the flames grew larger and more voracious, threatening to engulf the historic old building. Mercifully, a light rain had saturated the roof of the Lodge and the large trees in front of it, which kept the fire from spreading, as did quick action by local firefighters. After struggling with inadequate water pressure and incompatible couplings between their hoses and the Lodge's main water line, the firefighters dropped an auxiliary pump into the swimming pool. When the pump floated like a cork, local teenager Howdy Fry jumped in to hold it under the water. Other engines quickly put several more pumps in the pool, and with thousands of gallons of water now at their disposal, firefighters hacked two holes through the Lodge roof and unleashed a furious counterattack against the flames from above.

The effect was nearly immediate. The curtain of water from the swimming pool quickly extinguished the flames, creating enormous plumes of black smoke that could be seen

Local teenager Howdy Fry jumped fully-clothed into the Grand Lake Lodge swimming pool to hold down a large pump supplying water to desperate firefighters. Water from the pool played a decisive role in the battle to contain the fire. (Courtesy James family, Grand Lake Lodge)

for miles around. Bob Scott remembered everyone on the front lawn clapping at this fortuitous turn of events. The Grand Lake Lodge had been saved, but the building paid a heavy price. The fire charred nearly every inch of the beautiful hand-peeled logs supporting the structure, melted most of the light fixtures and restaurant glassware, and destroyed much of the valuable taxidermy collection. In addition, the kitchen roof had caved in, the dining room roof had two gaping holes through it, and anything not scorched by the flames suffered heavy smoke and water damage. The James family had no choice but to close the Lodge for the rest of the summer. Employees were given the choice of staying on the property and working at the Trail Ridge Store or returning home. Many left, but a few dedicated souls (including Bob Scott) chose to stay, cooking their meals in an outdoor kitchen set up under a makeshift lean-to roof. Scott remembered weeks and weeks of hamburgers every night.

Tangled hoses supply water to firefighters battling the blaze at the rear of the Lodge kitchen, where the fire started. The melted remains of the clerestory can be seen to the left of the man standing on the roof in the upper center of the photograph. (Courtesy James family, Grand Lake Lodge)

For the next seven years the Grand Lake Lodge remained closed to the public, but every summer a new batch of college students arrived to work at the Trail Ridge Store. These employees lived in the guest cabins at the Lodge and rode a bus (affectionately known as "Hoss") every morning to work. A small crew did maintenance work around the property, and after about five years the James family decided to initiate renovations on the main building. A handful of young men began the long and arduous task of re-peeling all of the blackened logs, from one end of the building to the other. The legendary Larry Hegeman did the lion's share of the work, using a sharp draw knife to scrape off layers of charred wood. Most of the peeled logs in the Grand Lake Lodge exhibit his handiwork.

As work progressed on the log peeling, the infamous "Burned-Out Ballroom" slowly began to take shape in the

A dining room table set for a dinner that was never served.
(Courtesy James family, Grand Lake Lodge)

lobby. A temporary plywood barrier blocked access to the most seriously damaged portion of the building, so employees cleaned up the the lobby area and transformed it into a first-rate, multipurpose party emporium, complete with a bar (the Front Desk) and loud rock and roll shaking soot from the rafters. Ted James Jr. even purchased a supply of used roller skates, which magically transformed the lobby into a roller rink. The Burned-Out Ballroom became Ground Zero for employee functions and eventually achieved mythical status in Grand Lake Lodge lore. Old-timers still grin with a twinkle in their eyes when asked about those days.

BACK IN BUSINESS

In the summer of 1980 the Grand Lake Lodge once again welcomed guests, albeit on a limited basis. The main building remained closed except for the Front Desk, but some of the cabins had been opened for overnight accommodations. The next summer the entire property officially reopened, much to the delight of loyal customers. Ted James Jr. continued to direct operations despite having lost his eyesight to cancer

The Lodge's fully functional, 1931 Ford Pumper Truck, an important component of the post-fire prevention program at the Grand Lake Lodge. This vehicle is also a perennial favorite during the Buffalo Barbecue Days Parade. (Courtesy James family, Grand Lake Lodge)

in early 1981, and renowned local restaurateur David McDougal agreed to lease the kitchen and dining room operation. Upgrades included new exhaust hoods and fire suppression equipment for the grill area, as well as an abundance of fire extinguishers. McDougal's expertise gave the James family an opportunity to concentrate on the hotel side of the business. The Burned-Out Ballroom became a faded memory, replaced by a completely restored lobby boasting new taxidermy, Indian rugs, and hand-crafted furniture. Hand-peeled logs charred black by the fire appeared brand new, while an improved electrical system and new light fixtures gave the entire building a soft, warm glow. Under the capable guidance of Sue James, the Gift Shop reopened with new merchandise, and expensive cabin upgrades greeted the first new guests. After seven long years, the Grand Lake Lodge was back in business.

Evoking memories of the past, three Ford Model A's welcome visitors to the Grand Lake Lodge. The beautifully-restored fleet consists of a 1929 pickup, a 1929 Woodie Wagon, and the flagship, a 1928 Phaeton convertible. (Courtesy Denise M. Sheffer)

Repairs and cabin renovations continued throughout the 1980s and into the 1990s. Maintenance alone consumed an enormous amount of revenue. Electrical, sewer, and plumbing systems had to be updated to comply with the latest codes. Long winters and heavy snow loads caused new leaks and cracked roads every spring, creating monumental headaches for maintenance and grounds crews. Increased business meant increased wear and tear on old furniture and equipment, much of which had to be repaired or replaced every few years. Still, the James family remained committed to the property, and through their quiet perseverance and diligent work the Grand Lake Lodge continued to improve. Official acknowledgement of their dedication came in 1993 when the United States Department of the Interior listed the Grand Lake Lodge in the National Register of Historic Places. The designation recognized the Lodge's significant contribution to the preservation of the "Rocky Mountain

The view from the Grand Lake Lodge, circa 1965. The pool has since been completely renovated to include a twelve-person hot-tub, and lush green lawns now cover the old roadway. (Courtesy James family, Grand Lake Lodge)

rustic stick" style of architecture once so prevalent in national parks throughout the American West.

As a National Historic Landmark, the Grand Lake Lodge takes great pride in being one of the few surviving structures from the early days of Colorado tourism. The Lodge's fleet of classic Ford Model A's evokes memories of those early days, when tourism was still a great adventure. While a few concessions to modern technology have been made (a new hot tub, satellite TV in the bar), the Lodge remains committed to preserving the integrity of its historic designation. Sadly, both Ted Sr. and Ted Jr. have passed away, but three generations of the James family continue to be proudly involved in the operation of the facility.

Aerial view of the Grand Lake Lodge, looking north toward the Never Summer Mountains. The seventy-acre property is bordered on three sides by Rocky Mountain National Park and features staggering views of the entire Grand Lake region. 1995 photo. (Courtesy James family, Grand Lake Lodge)

A NOTE ON SOURCES

Those seeking further information on the history of Grand Lake should first consult the two books written by Mary Lyons Cairns: *Grand Lake: The Pioneers* (Denver: The World Press, Inc., 1946) and *Grand Lake in the Olden Days* (Frederick, CO.: Renaissance House Publishers, 1971). Both texts are filled with rare photographs and indispensable information on the people and events that helped shape Grand Lake's formative years. Though considerably less detailed, Caroline Bancroft's *Grand Lake: From Utes to Yachts* (Boulder: Johnson Publishing Co., 1968) and *Estes Park and Grand Lake: Romantic History of the Trail Ridge Towns* (Boulder: Johnson Publishing Co., 1968) also contain some interesting nuggets of historical information, as does Nell Pauly's *Ghosts of the Shootin'* (Grand Lake, CO., 1961).

Robert C. Black's *Island in the Rockies* (Boulder: Pruett Publishing Co., 1969) is the definitive history of Grand County. Beautifully written, meticulously researched, Black's book is the best source for factual data on Grand Lake or any other community in Middle Park. The text is extensively footnoted and includes both a comprehensive index and an exhaustive bibliography. As a research tool, this book is simply unsurpassed. Nearly as impressive is C.W. Buchholtz's *Rocky Mountain National Park: A History* (Boulder: Colorado Associated University Press, 1983), which contains a great deal of information on Grand Lake. The text is supplemented by ample footnotes and an excellent bibliographical essay. Enos Mills' *The Rocky Mountain National Park* (Boston: Houghton Mifflin, 1932) offers wonderful insights from the man most responsible for the park's creation.

Another outstanding source is *High Country Names* (Boulder: Johnson Books, 1994) by Louisa Ward Arps and Elinor Eppich Kingery, which contains an astonishing amount of information about the origins of names in the Rocky Mountain National Park region. The 1966 edition of this work also includes a number of historic photographs. Richard Barth's *Pioneers of the Colorado Parks* (Caldwell, Idaho: Caxton Printers, 1997) is an easy-to-read summary of some of the seminal events in the history of Middle Park. Information on the Ute Indians can be found *in People of the Shining Mountains* (Boulder: Pruett Publishing Co., 1982) by Charles S. Marsh, while Dan Tyler's *The Last Water Hole in the West* (Niwot, CO.: University Press of Colorado, 1992) is the best source for facts on the Colorado-Big Thompson Project. Those seeking information on John Wesley Powell should start with Wallace Stegner's *Beyond The Hundredth Meridian* (Boston: Houghton Mifflin, 1954; reprint, New York: Penguin Books, 1992), while those interested in William Henry Jackson should consult *The Diaries of William Henry Jackson*, edited by LeRoy and Ann Hafen (Glendale, CA.: The Arthur H. Clark Co., 1959), and *Time Exposure: The Autobiography of William Henry* Jackson (New York: G. P. Putnam's Sons, 1940).

Newspaper and journal articles containing information on the history of Grand Lake are abundant. The best source is the *Grand Lake Prospector*, although copies of this short-lived newspaper are hard to come by. The Colorado Historical Society has a limited number of editions. Other newspapers to consult are the Georgetown *Colorado Miner*, the Hot Sulphur Springs (later Kremmling) *Middle Park Times*, the Fraser *Grand County Citizen*, the Teller *North Park Miner*, the *Denver Post,* and the Denver *Rocky Mountain News*. For journal articles, *The Colorado Magazine* is far and away the best source.

Various historical society publications also contain information on the history of Grand Lake, including several by the Rocky Mountain Nature Association, the Grand Lake Area Historical Society, and the Grand County Historical Association. The Colorado Historical Society and the Denver Public Library, Western History Collection, have extensive historical archives containing rare manuscripts and photographs pertaining to Grand

Lake. The DPL historic photo database is especially impressive.

In addition to the texts, articles, and documents listed, the best sources of information on the history of Grand Lake are the long-time residents and visitors who enjoy sharing their memories of the past. The information they possess is priceless, and accessing it usually requires little more than expressing a genuine interest in hearing their stories. Such stories rarely disappoint.

Finally, a cautionary note. The written and oral historical records of Grand Lake are rife with contradictions and discrepancies concerning facts such as names, dates, spelling, and chronological sequence. Different versions of the same story often contain unverifiable claims, exaggerations, and just plain misinformation. When confronted with such anomalies, I tended to rely on the texts that have the best footnotes, which in the case of Grand Lake happen to be Black's *Island in the Rockies* and Buchholtz's *Rocky Mountain National Park: A History.* Although these two books do not focus specifically on the history of Grand Lake, they contain enough detailed documentation to clarify most discrepancies in the historical record.